ARTIFICIAL INTELLIGENCE

Dive into the Deep Insight of Artificial Intelligence. Find Out About the Impact of AI Coming into Our Daily Lives and How to Survive and Dominate the AI System as Human Beings.

By Freddie Slater

Artificial Intelligence

Table of Contents

Artificial Intelligence

Introduction

Artificial intelligence is progressing rapidly in our daily life with new advanced innovations day in day out. Computer science systems are designed to perform small instant tasks, facial recognition, self-driving cars, and performance of other minor duties. However, artificial intelligence primarily develops advanced and more complex systems that would outperform humans in whatever way possible. These are including the performance of more complicated tasks like solving problems and playing chess. Therefore, the goal of AI in the future is to perfect all human activities and provide better solutions to problems than humans normally do. An automated system that is capable of doing all the human functions from controlling cars to computerized business systems, in the long term, will pose many different challenges. Moreover, during the prevention of the development of lethal arms that possibly harm humans once they are used to attack. As a result of which the development of super Artificial Intelligence that undergoes self-improvement, triggering an intelligence explosion would leave the human intellectual capacity by far. Super AI development will make history by marking the greatest inventions. Consequently, the invention of highly advanced technologies has significantly supported in war eradication, developing appropriate prevention measures, and proper means of fighting diseases.

Most interestingly, new AI-based advanced technologies would help a lot in fighting against poverty. We have been studying Artificial Intelligence (AI) for decades, and it is still one of the most elusive subjects in Computer Science. And this is partly the reason for how large and nebulous the subject is. Artificial intelligence is ranging from thinkable machines to search algorithms that are used to play board games. Its applications are visible in almost every way computers are used in our society. The development of technology has significantly advanced since the 1990s with added functionalities and a further improvement in every way of life. Early before the 1990s, artificial intelligence was considered as fiction, but since the 1990s, the concept of AI as an area of science is no more considered as a fiction concept. Now, it has become our daily life reality. Machine learning using neural networks mimic the actual processes of the real neurons. Artificial intelligence allows machines to process complex data and provide accurate results and information. With the development and innovations of artificial intelligence marks the golden age. AI is now the most advanced technology widely used in our daily life. Hence, artificial intelligence will dominate the focus of technology for the next decades with improved added functionalities.

Notice that AI has improved the lives of people today, and living with AI is living the best. It should further be noted that AI technology integration has a great connectedness to improve people's activities in their everyday life.

In this artificially intelligent book, you will get the opportunity to learn and understand everything you need to know about artificial intelligence. From its historical fictional concepts and theory to practice, highlighting its benefits, fall to rise happenings, and how it is impacting our daily life.

History of Artificial Intelligence

Artificial intelligence

John McCarthy in 1956, coined the term Artificial Intelligence during his first academic conference on the subject. Though, the journey of understanding of thinkable machines began much before that. About Vannevar Bush's seminal work, we may think that he proposed such a system that amplifies people's own understand and knowledge. Alan Turing, after 5 years, wrote a paper on the notion of intelligent machines that are capable of simulating human beings. The computer's ability to logic processing cannot be refuted by someone. Still, many don't know and even haven't imagined if a machine can think. It is important and even crucial for people to know the precise definition of *think* because there has been some strong opposition as to whether this notion is even possible or not. A 'Chinese room' argument is the best so-called example of this. The imagination of someone who is locked in a room, where they were passed notes in Chinese using an entire library of rules & look-up tables, and they would be able enough to produce valid responses in Chinese. The question here is that, would they really understand the Chinese language? Based on the argument, since computers would always be applying rote fact lookup, and could never understand a subject.

Many researchers refuted this argument in numerous ways, but it does undermine the faith of people in machines & so-called expert systems in different life-critical applications.

At the AI Dartmouth summer research project, McCarthy organized a workshop in 1956 in which Artificial Intelligence (AI) was officially born and christened as a field. Investigation of ways in which machines could be made to simulate aspects of intelligence was considered as the goal of this project—the focused and essential idea that continue driving the field forward. In the proposal, McCarthy co-authored for the workshop along with Nathaniel Rochester, Marvin Minsky, and Claude Shannon. The overall credit goes to the team, but McCarthy is well-known for the use of the term Artificial Intelligence and is credited with it. Among the attendants, many people started working and led significant projects under the banner of AI. These great people were passionate about AI, including Arthur Samuel, Selfridge, Oliver, Ray Solomonoff, Herbert Simon, and Allen Newell.

A dedicated research community and a unified identity for the AI field was created at the Dartmouth workshop, many of the technical ideas that have come to describe Artificial Intelligence existed much earlier.

Thomas Bayes, in the 18th century, provided a framework for reasoning about the **probability** of events. George Boole, in the 19th century, showed that **logical reasoning**—dating back to Aristotle—could be performed systematically in such a manner similar to solving a system of equations. By the turn of the 20th century, experimental sciences progress had led to the emergence of the **statistics** field, with the help of which inferences from data to be drawn rigorously. The idea of engineering a machine physically and sequences of instructions to be executed, the imagination of pioneers was captured, such as Charles Babbage. By the early 1950s, this had matured and resulted in the construction of the first **electronic computers**. Primitive **robots** known for their ability to sense and act autonomously had also been built by that time.

One of the most influential ideas and contributions that underpin Computer Science becomes possible with the help of Alan Turing. Alan Turing proposed a formal model of computing. Turing's classic essay, Computing Intelligence, and Machinery, the possibility of computers is imagined, which is created for simulating intelligence and explores many of the ingredients that are now associated with AI. These include how intelligence can possibly be tested and how machines could learn automatically. AI is inspired by these ideas. Though Turing had no access to the computing resources that are needed for the translation of his ideas into action.
Several focal areas in the quest for Artificial Intelligence emerged between the two decades from the 1950s to the 1970s.

Simon and Newell pioneered the foray into **heuristic search**. Heuristic search is an efficient procedure for finding solutions in large and combinatorial spaces. They particularly applied this idea to construct proofs of mathematical theorems. This was done firstly through their Logic Theorist program, and then through the General Problem Solver. Early work in character recognition in the area of **computer vision**, by Selfridge & colleagues, laid the basis for more complex applications such as face recognition. Also, work on **natural language processing (NLP)** had begun by the late 60s. "Shakey" is a wheeled robot that built at SRI International, and the field of **mobile robotics** launched with it. The checkers-playing program by Samuels improved itself through self-play. This happened to be one of the first working instances of a **machine learning** system. Rosenblatt's Perceptron is a computational model that is based on biological neurons that occurred as the basis for the field of **artificial neural networks (ANNs)**. Building the **expert systems** were advocated by Feigenbaum and others—knowledge repositories tailored for specialized domains such as medical diagnosis and chemistry.

The early conceptual progress assumes explicitly the presence of a symbolic system that could be possibly reasoned about and built upon. But by the early 1980s, in spite of this promising headway made into different aspects of AI. Still, no significant practical successes could be boosted by the field. This gap between practice and theory arose in part from a deficient emphasis within the Artificial Intelligence community physically on grounding systems with direct access to environmental data and signals. There was also an overemphasis on (True/False) known as the Boolean logic, that is overlooking the requisite to quantify uncertainty. In the mid-1980s, when the interest of people in Artificial Intelligence dropped and funding dried up, the field was forced to take cognizance of these shortcomings. This period is called "AI winter" By Nilsson.

A much-needed resurgence in the 1990s built upon the idea that "Good Old-Fashioned AI" was inadequate to building intelligent systems as an end-to-end approach. Rather, intelligent systems necessary to be built from the ground up, at all times, solving the task at hand, albeit with many different degrees of proficiency. Technological progress had also been making the task of building systems that are driven by real-world data feasibly. Reliable and cheaper hardware for actuation and sensing made robots easier to build Further, the capacity of the internet to gather large amounts of data, and the availability of computing storage and power to process that data, enabled statistical techniques and ways that derive solutions from data by design. These developments have allowed Artificial Intelligence to emerge over the past two decades as a profound impact on our daily lives, which we will be covering later in detail.

Expert Systems

Overview

Expert systems are those computer programs that aim to model human expertise in multiple specific knowledge areas. Expert systems have usually three basic components: a knowledge database with rules and facts that represent human experience and knowledge, an inference engine processing consultation, and to determine how inferences are being made, an output/input interface to interact with the users.

According to K. S. Metaxiotis et al., characteristics of expert systems are:

- Not just use numerical calculations but also symbolic logic;
- With data-driven processing;
- a knowledge database containing explicit contents of a certain area of knowledge; &
- Capable of interpreting conclusions in such a way that it is easier for users to understand.

In the early 1950s, Expert systems first emerged as a subset of AI when the Rand-Carnegie team developed the general problem solver for dealing with geometric problems, theorems proof, and chess playing. John McCarthy at MIT, at the same time, later on, invented LISP, the later dominant programming language in expert systems and Artificial Intelligence.

The expert systems were increasingly used in industrial applications during the 1960s and1970s. Let's know about some of the famous applications during this decade were MYCIN (a medical diagnosis system), DENDRAL (a chemical structure analyzer), ACE (AT&T's cable maintenance system), and XCON (a computer hardware configuration system). In 1972, PROLOG was created as an alternative to LISP in logic programming designed to handle computational linguistics, especially NLP (natural language processing). Artificial Intelligence was perceived as a direct threat to humans at that time because expert systems were considered revolutionary solutions capable of solving problems in any area of human activity. This perception was built that would later bring an inevitable skeptical backlash. These successful systems stimulated a near-magical fascination with smart applications. The industry largely deemed the expert systems as a competitive tool to sustain technological advantages. By the end of the 1980s, 500 companies were involved in either maintaining or developing expert systems. Expert systems usage improved with a growth rate of 30% a year. Companies like TI, IBM, DEC, Xerox, HP, and universities such as Stanford, MIT, Carnegie-Mellon, Rutgers, and many more had taken part in pursuing expert system technology & developing practical applications.

Expert systems have expanded nowadays into many sectors of our society and can be found in a broad spectrum of areas such as credit authorization, health care, chemical analysis, financial management, corporate planning, genetic engineering, oil and mineral prospecting, automobile manufacture and design, and air-traffic control.

As K. S. Metaxiotis and colleagues pointed out that the importance of expert systems is increasing in both decision support, which provides options and issues to decision-makers, and decision making where people can make decisions beyond their level of experience and knowledge. Expert systems have distinct leads over traditional computer programs. Expert systems, in contrast to humans, can provide permanent storage for expertise and knowledge; once programmed to use and ask for inputs, it offers a consistent level of consultation; and provide support as a depository of knowledge from potentially unlimited expert sources and thereby provide support in the comprehensive decisions.

Key Technological Issues

Numerous unresolved technical performance limitations and issues that severely affect the implementation and development of expert systems. The most critical of these problems confronting institutions and corporations and the solutions thereof will be examined in this section.

The major technological issues facing expert systems lie in the areas of *software methodology and standards,* handling uncertainty, knowledge acquisition, and validation.

Software Standards and Interoperability: there is no general standard in development methodology and expert system software, neither commonly adopted expert system infrastructure and protocols exist. The knowledge system is developed uniquely with a little consideration for interoperability. With the coalition of the American Association of Artificial Intelligence (AAAI), DARPA, the IEEE Computer Society, and the US government, recent efforts in defining expert system standards have been actively pursued. Development complexity, risks, and costs could be reduced once widely accepted standards are established, and also the expert system new generation tools are in place. *Knowledge Acquisition and Analysis* is usually considering a way to discover the static facts of the world and the relationships of many different events that human performs in solving real-life problems. Human's problem-solving skills oftentimes are far more complex and complicated than what the knowledge collection can achieve. Let's consider an example; humans at an early age normally learn how to walk sometimes through practices and sometimes painful experiences. This kind of

error know-how and trial is not accessible in the form of rules and facts.
Asking a human to articulate a set of rules based on their know-how, mainly the reflection of skills, will not be accurate. Furthermore, knowledge systems do not learn from their experience.

You might have heard about the Case-based reasoning (CBR) theory. This theory focuses on solving new problems that are based on similar past problem solutions. This seems to be capable of eliminating the complex task of maintaining facts and rules using the adaptive acquisition of problem-solving techniques. CBR does not handle to assemble and process commonsense knowledge, and therefore the CYC project developed by Cycorp Inc. aims to handle this. The expert systems in the future could integrate the commonsense knowledge from the CYC project with the application-specific modules to be captured from CBR for the enhancement of their analysis process and knowledge acquisition.

Handling Uncertain Situation; Due to the lacking of precision in inputs and rules, the ability of expert systems to derive correct output is often compromised. The inference engine builts upon algorithms manipulating knowledge in the form of a decision tree that is not designed to handle uncertainty. Some expert systems incorporate fuzzy logic to cope with imprecise inputs and rules in areas such as linear and nonlinear control, financial systems, pattern recognition, and data analysis. Present labels are usually used by the fuzzy logic in such systems to categorize real-time inputs, and utilizes fuzzy inference in calculating numerical outputs and conclusions from imprecise rules. *System Integration* Knowledge database has no easy access. The LISP-based expert system tools lack the ability to integrating with other applications that are written in traditional languages. You should know that most of the systems are still not portable among different hardware. Such issues of system integration can contribute to higher risks and costs. For this, the requirement of new system architectures can fully integrate knowledge databases and external systems. *Validation*, expert systems quality is often measured with its comparison to the results of those derived from human experts. However, there are ambiguous validation or verification techniques specifications. Adequate evaluation of an expert system remains an open question, although several attempts have been made in utilizing pre-established test cases that are developed by independent experts in verifying the reliability and performance of the systems.

Managerial and Organizational Challenges

Successes in the economic or technical sense of an expert system do not guarantee long-term use or a high-level of adoption rate in businesses. During the early and the middle of the 1980s, expert systems built as surveyed by T. Grandon Gill. The key results of all the systems surveyed were as follows:

- about 1-3rd were being actively maintained and used
- about 1-6th were though available to users but were not being maintained, and
- about one-half were abandoned.

This survey indicated another problem, which was the problems suffered by some of those machines that fell into disuse had neither an economic nor technical basis. *Alignment of Technology and Business Strategy* a substantial amount of

investments and efforts are also involved in building expert systems. Inconsistency between the technology and the organization's business strategy could ultimately ruin such efforts and money.

Maintenance Cost of Expert Systems We know that expert systems are complicated and can require extensive knowledge of development tools developed and maintained by people and the application domain, so ultimately, the maintenance cost could be high in this case. A loss of key personnel results in almost the full portion of the project to be re-worked. Keep in mind that projects can be delayed or abandoned if the vulnerabilities in staffing turnover are unresolved. *Expert Systems Make Mistakes* there will be legal concerns over "expert system makes mistakes," which could drive developers and investors away. Remind what we mentioned previously, there is consensus on what testing is essential for evaluating an expert system's reliability, validity, and performance. There is not even a single legal authority to validate and certify systems. The potential functional and legal liabilities of such systems go wrong, especially in life-critical systems such as air-traffic control and medical diagnosis could be astronomical and crippling. *Resistance from Users* as we know that traditional computer programs cannot perform tasks better than the expert systems, but expert systems perform tasks just like an expert performs. This could trigger strong resistance and opposition to such technology from users with concerns about expert systems replacing them and taking their jobs. These organizational and managerial challenges appear to be very crucial for expert systems.. When it comes to the failure of taking care of such issues, it could lead to system cancellation or abandonment.

Is "Thinking" Machine Ever Possible

It was a long dream of scientists that a system could "think" autonomously free of human interference. Even the five decades of research were not enough to bring this dream come true. The human beings intuitive intelligence is still beyond the capabilities of 'reasoning machines.' Some people are more optimistic, while some deem the discovery of a 'thinkable machine' a dangerous endeavor that is ultimately doomed to failure. Jeff Hawkins, in his award-winning book "On Intelligence," predicted that the mind-machine might appear its existence in the world within a decade. His reason for this prediction was, "It took fifty years to switch from room-sized computers to pocket size. In comparison to this, as we are now in an advanced technological position, it should go much faster for the same transition for intelligent machines." For exploring expert systems development potential, it is essential for comparing the differences between machine "thinking" and humans, and discussion on their possibilities for the future.

Human's Know-how and Intuitive Intelligence

You might remember the example that we mentioned previously about humans who learn how to walk through practice and trial, and such skill is called "know-how." Humans acquire these skills through experiences and instructions. As we know that the human learning process is actually a gradual process, and there is appearing to have no sudden leaping forward that is from rule-based knowledge to experience-based know-how. Novices follow the instructions and rules, while more competent users take into account the situation elements like sensing the opponent's weakness in chess play. Very proficient users recall past solutions of similar experience and can intuitively apply them to the present without first sorting them out by going through rule-based deliberations or rules. Another aspect of human intelligence is the different mindset when they consciously work on solving problems. Chess play as an example; grand maters do not see themselves as board manipulating pieces. Rather, they involved themselves deeply in the world of opportunities, strengths, threats, weaknesses, hopes, and fears. With this involvement level, human experts to think differently and come up with innovative solutions and new innovations.

The Human Mind

Properties of the human brain are very interesting. Speculation of Raj Reddy says that the human brain is composed of about one hundred billion neural cells, and normally there is a possibility that the brain might be performing over 200 trillion operations every second if not faster than that. In problem domains such as speech, motor processes, and vision, "it is more powerful than one thousand supercomputers; however, it is less powerful than a 4-bit microprocessor when it comes to simple tasks such as multiplication." These processing events going on in the brain need little conscious awareness and effort the part of humans, and their emulation is extremely difficult for machines. In contrast, machines can excel in some processes that are difficult and possible for a human being. Reddy went on to argue that if a silicon-based intelligence is ever achieved, after all, it might just have different attributes.

Hubert Dreyfus and colleagues also questioned if the mind of a human can be materialized into an info-processing machine. An example might tell you how, "if it is known that a small box is resting on a large box, it can be imagined what would happen if the large box is removed." However, a computer must be given a list of facts about boxes, such as their weight, size, and frictional coefficients, details, or information about how each is affected by various kinds of movements."

Generally, a human thinks with images, and this what we know "imagination." Human beings do not think the descriptions but use images to respond and understand situations. Unlike logic machines step-by-step reasoning, the human process is totally different from such explicit.

What the Future Holds

The dream of a "thinkable" machine could be controversial, exciting, and also intimidating. In the book "*The Singularity Is Near,"* Ray Kurzweil says that *When Humans Transcend Biology* provides some intriguing future thoughts such as the nanobots, which are sub-micro agents injected into the human bloodstream. They could be brought in use for monitoring and maintaining biological and chemical balances. In addition to this, these nanobots could also specialize patrolling the brain and downloading synaptic connections and every stored neural pattern from brain cells to a supercomputer system. A system like these would, in turn, recreate a version of software of the human mind, including emotions, memory, instincts, and thoughts. Also, there is a possibility of porting the program to other machines just like any other software, acting and thinking as "yourself" with immortality! Unambiguously, the human mind from inside or the inner-workings are more complicated, complex, and challenging to start creating machines that could simulate human intellectual abilities is daunting. Furthermore, it still remains debatable on endowing computer systems possibility with human-like intelligence.

The debate has extended beyond whether machines can "think" like humans. If the dream of "thinkable" machines become a reality, then undoubtedly, this would have profound social implications and cause permanent changes in the very foundation of the society we are living in. Nevertheless, the current success of expert systems seems assured.

Social Implications of Expert Systems

To harness the brainpower of the experts could be passed along in assisting others have always been the major driving force behind the expert systems development. It is among the most positive potentials of Artificial Intelligence. As mentioned by Reddy, "to share the know-how and knowledge in the form of information products is the only way that supports in reducing this ever-widening gap between the have and have-nots." Expert systems could be used as a mean of sharing the wealth of knowledge; the wealth of sharing with the disadvantaged is of great importance. As progress has been made to develop smart AI applications, we might be doing well on our way to "help the illiterate, the poor, and the disadvantaged people of all the nations and the world." While expert systems, when it comes to its usage, is of great importance and benefit to our social lives, there are also determinants and potential downfalls that could lead to ethical and extremely difficult legal dilemmas.

While it is obviously foolhardy and dangerous to deploy logic machines used as a command on the battlefield, think about the system of air-traffic control that is used to route airplanes carrying hundreds and thousands of passengers or used in the systems of medical diagnosis that might assist physicians in death-or-life situations?

What can possibly happen as of result of the wrong advice of these systems? Accountability does not make sense because who should be held accountable? Furthermore, when it comes to systems that think autonomously and are aware of their own existence, could they be advicing incorrectly and whether that is intentional or not? In the future, do you think the legal system should be extended to deal with machines, just as in Isaac Asimov's fiction "Three Laws of Robotics"?

Expert systems development also raises the question of who should own the knowledge, and there should be an owner. A list of questions was presented by Richard L Dunn on this issue: "Is it your employer, or you? How much should you share with a knowledge engineer who shows up at your office? Is your value more or less to your company if he 'drains your brain'? Is your company allowed to take that intelligence and give it away or sell it to someone else or a party without compensating you?" Certainly, intellectual property laws and copyrights are well established.

It is essential for employers to own the copyrightable materials and patentable products developed during an employment career. But with regard to the experience and knowledge you have gained during work, are they subjected to the same regulation? And after all, personal experience and knowledge are marketable commodities. Therefore, that is the reason for your hiring by your employer. However, supposing that experience or knowledge could somehow be stored and captured in a computer system that you no longer control, or that computer system has acquired experience and knowledge from a group of people or someone else who have the same expertise like you, does the company still need your services? It would be better to get prepared for all these questions before it gets too late to answer them.

The human intelligence complexities had been underestimated before, especially when it comes to the field of expert systems. Managerial challenges and technological limitations still remain in expert systems development. However, the future for expert systems seems bright with the success of neural networks despite the earlier setbacks, CASE technology, and other state-of-art technologies. Furthermore, careful consideration must be given to ethical and legal issues that will certainly arise during the advancement of expert system technology. Should the dream of autonomous "thinkable" machines ever become a reality, our lives as we know it would be changed forever?

Uses of AI in our Daily Life

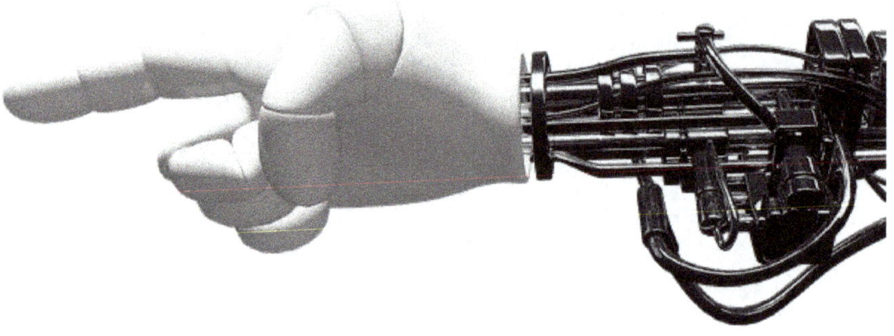

We all use artificial intelligence in our lives daily in many ways. We use it, manage it, and respond to AI all the time, every hour and every minute of the day.

Lack of skilled workforce in the industry, it is required for businesses to use AI. Companies hire programmers who create specific tasks to automate the workforce with the help of machines and software.

Let's understand, manage and use AI in a practical way.

1. Automate the repetitive tasks

AI brings friendly changes in any kind of operation by making it faster and reliable. For repetitive tasks like social media Blog sharing on specified times, schedules Post for publishing are all made easy by AI.

For example, the recurring monthly deposits into your bank accounts, automatic bills payments, automatic credit recharges, etc. these simple tasks consume our time, and AI is used to help us complete these tasks without wasting our time.

2.**AI enables this method, "Let Machine Play Your Roles".**

Jobs like production, recycling, cleaning, infrastructure development, design, transport, and many engineering jobs are mostly done by AI Machines. These machines are smart, they collect data and information, and they are able to make their own decisions.

3 decades ago, all these jobs were done by humans using machines manually, but AI has replaced them as they are more reliable, and there is less chance of error. These machines

collect data and information, and it is processed and analyzed to make the job more efficient.

AI or Automation is programmed on the basis of the following methods.

i) Users behavior prediction

Notice how search engines offer a suggestion to complete your sentences? When a user input and inquiry into the algorithmic machines, it will predict what the user may want to type. This means that the search engine is programmed to similar search, responsive websites automatically adapt based on user devices. This means website designs (CSS) are already programmed to keep the user interface and user experience the same on any device.

You must be thinking of how anyone can predict some once future behavior. It is true no one can tell the future, but AI is coming close to it, would you like to know how it's happening?

All of this is made possible by the data collected by each machine and applications that we are using in our daily lives. The pattern of data collected by the machines and user behavior is analyzed by computers and people. And this is why they are programming the future by using programming languages to collect, manage and analyze all sorts of data and create automatic outputs for the future.

ii) Faster data collection methods and analysis methods.

Everything from a gauging machine to a heartbeat checking gadget. A PC is firing up or closing down. From turning the information in a portable on and off. Nearly everything that you use, work, purchase, sell, watch, search, like, install, transfer, and so forth, every one of these procedures makes and produce information.

So these are the information assortment and Analyses strategies being utilized by organizations and items to make counterfeit customized gadgets and applications with the goal that machines can do your job.

iii) Innovation and development of hybrid computers.

A lot of data being produced by these assortment strategies requires adequate computing power, for it to be examined and managed. This is the place the advancement of hybrid PCs and innovation in technology is playing an important role. They have the raw processing capacity that can deal with a consistent stream of data continuously.

In case you're not capable yet of understanding AI use. Then understand what Data is and what is information?

In basic words, a collection of important facts that are produced by anything (people/electronic gadgets) is called data. An analysis of data brings forth information. Important and executable information is called data. And knowledge is the mix of important data and (information) analysis.

3. Use of AI in Automatic Graphics Designing.

Logo design, brochure plan, web designing, and a lot more illustrations parts are automatically designed, and such projects are already existing. You could simply utilize them. For instance, you need to make a logo for your organization, and the procedure is straightforward, type your organization name and choose category and search. Now select and payor download free. Same applies if you need a logo for IT consultancy organization, use the same process.

Presently, this is going on due to preexisting designs, portions of illustrations continuously make a shape dependent on your search query. The specialized thought is "Designs from search query". While it has started from the idea of a template, now it's used in our everyday life. We use it or not, however, we can't disregard it. Regardless of the quality, however, it's an innovative idea, and nearly everything in data innovation can turn out to be big in a couple of days.

4. AI Chat Bots, website chat plugins use in Customer Support/Sales Support Process

Chatting is a part of every individuals' everyday life. A large portion of the individuals is hooked on it. Today, programmed Chatbots are made on a similar theory, possible inquiry? The answer is already there and if you type "office space in Chicago", chatbots will say thanks for the information.

They will, at that point, communicate further and attempt to gather more data from you, like salesmen so they can recommend or sell the best item or service by narrowing down the extent of potential matches. In the end, they will send you a purchase link.

That is it. No person was there that you were talking with, that was a programmed function that is programmed based on possible queries from clients and answers to those inquiries and their conversation methods.

5. AI Notification

It's a fact that our modern life is driven by an excess of notifications and recommendations. Practically all applications, sites, and organizations are notifying you about your accessed networks, bought items, visited sites, commercials, and friends activities, and so on. Indeed, even these Sales/Marketing by organizations using AI are mostly on cell phones than PCs. Clients are under the objective of these AI applications. It's great until clients are not upset, baffled, disillusioned by these AI notifications and suggestion.

Clients are not only notified by AI but also compelled to make a decision. It doesn't make a difference if it's gainful or not. We do what needs to be done.

The negative side of AI use in our everyday life is that it's making us slaves. Telling you to invest more time on the website, to spend more money on internet business sites, to study certain causes and see increasingly more of what your friends are doing.

The arrangement is "you can just set priorities, what is urgent and important" in your everyday life and activities, and it should not be based on recommendations, notification and AI.

And yet, you can't Disregard AI use in day-to-day life absolutely. It's only that there are such a large number of advantages, and AI is the interest of time.

6. AI Promotional Email:

In our everyday life, we get a normally 5-10 special and programmed messages daily sent by organizations, sites, applications every day in my inbox, in light of my perusing history and activity on the Web. This is AI-based email marketing.

Each update isn't important. But it grabs our attention, and this is the goal of marketing organizations so that clients can click and purchase the services or products.

This is the use of AI in everyday life of web advertisers, digital marketing organizations, and almost every one of the applications. In simple words, the application is integrated with marketing automation, so it spares time, money for organizations and gets better revenue because the user is hooked on the internet shopping.

Personalized and contextual digital advertising

Artificial intelligence and machine mastering methods are used to be able to showcase and present personal ads and contextual ads on the user's display screen. AI tests user behaviors, device, location, source, community.

AI also tests software speed, responsiveness, layout, textual content size, images, and information. After the analysis involving users and platforms in a second, the AI-enabled signal displays ads automatically within the websites and apps, for example, blog website, social press websites, and apps.

Right now, several sides are receiving the benefits of this particular AI technology. Advertisers, Writers, and users. Users have become and receiving the details from the advertisement they will are looking for. And so they want to check out the source. Publishers are producing more revenue and visitors. And advertisers or businesses/companies are getting High RETURN and Conversion due in order to this.

The truth is usually that Machines, applications will be programmed in an approach so that they can generate goal-oriented content regarding customers/companies and at the particular same time generate this kind of revenue in quick time with the least expensive investment.

8. Auto-scaling based on website and apps traffic

The best majority associated with people uses the World Wide Web intended for watching videos, social networking, online learning, program deployment, building, editing, and collaboration together with the team member and even data storage in day-to-day life. The use associated with the internet in our existence is increasing by the particular day as more customers all over the world want to obtain the IT powers that will the internet holds.

Nevertheless, to access the strength it takes non-stop processing involving inputs and outputs upon the server. It needs a high-speed internet. It will require more quickly loading applications and internet sites so that the electric power is consistent and individuals are able to gain access to the AI advantages. two decades ago, you know the particular speed of sites, as properly as computers, was dismally low, and you can easily compare it today together with 4G -5G internet rates and 8-16GB RAM upon computers and phones.

Consequently to provide non-stop leisure, unlimited internet data bags, faster video streaming, and even video conferencing, fastest worldwide web speed for business in addition to online learning, course, plus degree programs for college students on website and programs, the newest concept in the particular market that takes almost everything from here to typically the next level by using Artificial intelligence is called fog up computing.

Cloud computing procedures and systems are developed on AI. In this specific, business, language schools, Federal. Agencies etc. can fix up remote infrastructure, distant data storage, backup, and event management, etc. The fog up infrastructure is programmed in the manner so that it can easily auto-scale its storage, acceleration, security and many even more things based on the particular load within the application.

in simple terms, if a hundred students (website & applications traffic) are using or even commanding the application to be able to perform the particular functioning, then Artificial intelligence instantly set the switch with the server to point M, if there are 3 hundred students in real-time intended for the same application that will auto-scale the storage space to Point C.

Right now because everything is functioning fast, no storage issue, no maintenance cost in addition to so forth it's quick and comfortable for those to be able to use the technology, is actually viable for business in order to integrated cloud computing in addition to artificial intelligence daily inside exchange of values covering up most of the portion of life.

In conclusion regarding the uses of Artificial Intelligence inside our daily lifestyle, we can say that will Artificial intelligence now altering our day to working day life to new criteria, methods, new routines, innovative healthy habits, new sorts of disease, the new kind associated with problems and solution. Many of us can say we're altering information technology again towards the new heights. In the particular past, there have been many changes, from the invention regarding the Internet to Look for Engine, social media marketing and advertising to online learning.

Advantages and Disadvantages of Artificial Intelligence

Nowadays with AI, machine studying and cloud computing, we are entering into a brand-new world when you locate self-driving cars, leading quality products, individualized applications, contextual and personalized alternatives, automatic fault finding and even troubleshooting, faster decision-generating (Business intelligence), innovative gardening, balanced diet scanning machines plus programs, increasing productivity, atmosphere protection methods, new ideas of face recognition, creativity in recycling, new types of business models that will help people to enhance and new theories that will be never thought involving before.

But these are usually just advantages of AI in our daily lifestyle. There is a reverse side too

AI's results are negative too, for instance, humans losing their work opportunities to machines and automatic programs, Also concerning is the fact machines, and applications will know your financial place, location, social circle, and many others.

Agents are your fresh virtual friend or store assistants, and since everything is definitely automated, it could finish up making many men and women less productive. Anxiety and stress may become the biggest issue for humans, which is definitely worse having a sedentary life-style that AI will present in the future. Individuals who have more specialized abilities and creativity throughout the world will turn into the most powerful region. Technically, data-driven world.

Artificial intelligence is like the boon for people within daily life when utilized right. But it features its own disadvantages also. Now this will rely on how much management of our minds many of us can provide to devices. How confident we have been of which technology will not help make us slaves.

Some great benefits of Artificial intelligence applications will be enormous and can better any professional sector. Why don't see some of these people

1) Reduction in Human Error:

The phrase "human error" was born mainly because humans make mistakes by time to time. Personal computers, yet , do not help make these mistakes if they happen to be designed properly. With Artificial brains, the decisions are obtained from the previously accumulated information applying a selected set of algorithms.

As result errors are reduced plus the chance of reaching out accuracy with an increased degree of precision is usually a possibility.

Example: Found in Weather Forecasting using AJAI they have reduced the particular majority of the human problems.

2) Takes risks instead of Humans:

This will be one of the greatest advantages of Artificial intelligence. We could overcome numerous risky limitations of people by developing an AJE Robot which can perform risky things with regard to us. Let it always be likely to mars, defuse the bomb, explore the biggest regions of oceans, mining intended for coal and oil, that can be used successfully in any kind regarding natural or man-made unfortunate occurrences.

Example: Seen about typically the Chernobyl nuclear engine electric power explosion in Ukraine? During that time there were no AI-powered robots that can aid us to minimize the particular result of radiation by simply manipulating the fire inside early stages, every man went close to typically the core was dead within a matter of a few minutes. They eventually poured fine sand and boron from micro helicopters from a mere length.

AI Robots can become used in such circumstances where intervention can always be hazardous.

3) Available 24x7:

A normal human will job for 4-6 hours a new day excluding the breaks or cracks. Humans are built on such a way to obtain time out for rejuvenating themselves and get prepared for a new day time of work and these people even have weekly offed to stay intact using their work-life and personal lifestyle. But using AI we all can make machines operate 24x7 without the breaks plus they don't even obtain bored, unlike humans.

Example: Educational Institutes and Helpline centres are getting several queries and issues which in turn can be handled successfully using AI.

4) Helping in Repetitive Jobs:

Throughout our day-to-day work, we all are performing many repeated works like sending a new thanking mail, verifying specific documents for errors in addition to many more things. Applying artificial intelligence, we are able to successfully automate these mundane duties and can even eliminate "boring" tasks for people and free them way up to be increasingly imaginative.

Example: In banks, all of us often see many verifications of documents to acquire a mortgage which is a repeating task for the proprietor of the bank. Working with AI Cognitive Automation typically, the owner can speed upward the verifying the files in which both the buyers and the owner will certainly be benefited.

5) Digital Assistance:

Some regarding the highly advanced agencies use digital assistants in order to interact with users, which usually saves the need with regard to recruiting. The digital co-workers also used in numerous websites to provide items that users want. We can easily talk with them about precisely what we are searching for. Many chatbots are designed consequently that it's become tough to determine that we are going to chatting with a chatbot or a human getting.

Example: We all realize that organizations have got a buyer support team that wants to clarify the uncertainties and queries of particular customers. Using AI, the particular organizations can create the Voice bot or Chatbot, which can help consumers using their queries. We all can see many companies already started with these people on their websites in addition to mobile applications.

6) Faster Decisions:

Using AI along with other technologies, we can easily make machines make choices faster when compared to a human, in addition, to carry out actions faster. While taking a selection human will analyze several factors both emotionally in addition to practically but AI-powered equipment ideal for what this is programmed and provides the results in a faster way.

Example: We all have played Mentally stimulating games in Windows. That is nearly impossible in order to beat CPU is typically the hard mode because involving the AI behind of which game. It will get the best possible step up a very short period according to the methods used behind it.

7) Daily Applications:

Daily programs, for example, Apple's Siri, Window's Cortana, Google's OK Search engines are often used in our own daily routine be it with regard to searching a location, going for a selfie, making a mobile phone call, replying to a new mail and many extras.

Example: Around 20 decades ago, while we happen to be planning to go someplace, we used to request a person who previously went there for particular directions. Great all we all have to do will be say "OK Google in which is Visakhapatnam". It will certainly demonstrate Visakhapatnam's location upon google map and the particular best path in your current way on the course to Visakhapatnam.

8) New Inventions:

AI is running many innovations in practically every domain, which may help humans solve the particular majority of complex difficulties.

Example: Recently, doctors could predict breast cancer within the woman at previous stages using advanced AI-based technologies. As every vivid side has a dark version in it.
Artificial Intelligence also has a few disadvantages.
Let's see many of them

1) High Costs of Creation:

As AI is updating every time, the hardware and computer software need to get up-to-date overtime to meet typically the latest requirements. Machines want repairing and maintenance, which in turn need plenty of expenses. Its creation needs huge costs as that they are very complex devices.

2) Making Humans Lazy:

AI is making people lazy with its software automating the majority associated with the work. Humans usually tend to get addicted to being able to these inventions, which could cause a problem to be able to future generations.

3) Unemployment:

As AI is upgrading the majority of typically the repetitive tasks and additional works with robots, human being interference is becoming significantly less, which will allow a major issue in the employment requirements. Every organization is seeking to change the minimum certified people with AI robots which often can do similar do the job with more efficiency.

4) No Emotions:

It will be obvious that machines are usually much better in terms of functioning efficiently, but they are unable to replace the human relationship that produces the team. Devices cannot create a bond along with humans, which can be a vital attribute when involves Staff Management.

5) Lacking Out of Box Thinking:

Devices can perform only all those tasks which they will be designed or programmed in order to do anything out regarding which they tend to drive or give irrelevant components which could become a significant backdrop.

These are generally several advantages and disadvantages associated with Artificial Intelligence. Every brand-new invention or breakthrough may have both, but all of us as humans need to be able to take care of which and make use of the positive factors of the invention to be able to create a better planet. Artificial intelligence has substantial potential advantages. The essential for humans will assure the "rise of the robots" doesn't get out regarding hand. Some people, in addition, say that Artificial intellect can destroy the human world if it goes directly into incorrect hands. But nevertheless, none of the AJE applications made at of which scale that can ruin or enslave humanity.

5 WAYS ARTIFICIAL INTELLIGENCE IS CHANGING ARCHITECTURE

The next measure of the latter is definitely Artificial General Intelligence. Thank goodness, our company is not here but. This sort of AI would end up being systems that may think just as well as us. Were about 30-40 years faraway from this. The key stage to remove from this specific form of AI is definitely it would learn plus upgrade itself, a demo and error learner.

Ultimately and most likely the coolest (scariest), occurs when AI updates itself to such some sort of level that it is higher than its human creators. This really is Artificial Super Intelligence. Even though some argue that all of us may never even attain this level on the particular AI scale, most would certainly agree that it will be possible. Artificial Nice Intelligence is what a person may see in a single associated with your favorite science fictional works movies.

So, let's have a look at the use of AJE in everyday life.

Smartphones

Let's get started with a gadget that you use daily, your smartphone. At this specific point, it truly is safe to be able to assume that both an individual and everyone in your own inner circle has the smartphone.

And, whether a person is realizing it or not really, you will be interacting with AJE every day. From your software, you download to the phone's own integrated software, each of these tools offers some layer of AJE weaved into their features.

Built-in smart assistants such as Google Assistant, Alexa, Siri, or Bixby use AJE to understand you and even to finish your recommended responsibilities. A number of the applications that a person uses like Spotify, Netflix, or Apple Music, use weak AI to best your listening experience, perhaps recommending the perfect track.

Even when you employ your beloved portrait setting to capture the excellent photo on your single-lens iPhone XR for Instagram, you are using AJAI to create that impact. More exciting features, just like mixed reality, are most also feasible because involving artificial intelligence.

Smart Homes and Their Devices

Each of our homes is getting a lot smarter, and you could thank artificial intelligence regarding that. The thing is definitely, our homes are merely going to get better. Smart speakers and appropriate appliances learn our behaviour over time with the particular try to make our life a lot cozier. There will come a new time in the around future, or maybe it is definitely already here once your house will know you much better than yourself. With AJAI since the driving force, your own home will be ready to predict when an individual wants to eat.

Your current preferred room temperature, if to turn the signals on and off about your home, when to be able to order groceries, and so forth

Transportation and Delivery

This might be a single of the more apparent examples. The rise involving the autonomous vehicle can easily be attributed to, yes, you guessed it, AJAI. Companies like Tesla possess brought the reality involving the self-driving vehicle directly into the forefront of tradition. However, the buck would not just stop there. The method that you get to work, no matter if it is through a tour bus or train, could turn into completely autonomous. In truth, a lot of organizations like GE and Toyota are banking on that. And let's not overlook that the way a person receives packages is established to improve too. Amazon and even Walmart are already making an investment in drone autonomous shipping and delivery programs.

Social Media:

You use social media each day, perhaps a bit too much. Though there has been a ton of controversy surrounding it, AI does have an impact on what you do, click-on, see and have interaction with on social media. AI takes all your past experience, internet searchers, interactions, and whole lot else that you do and tailors your social media experience just for you. In fact, this also makes your social media much more addictive.

VIDEOGAMES:

You likely clock in a few hours of gaming each day. Interestingly, AI is not best making video games greater exciting, but it's also permitting the manner of making games to be much less complicated and open for creators. Google and Nvidia are working on tremendous developer tools completely driven by powerful AI.

Banking and Finance:

From conducting inventory trades in nanoseconds or making suggestions for the excellent long-time period investment, AI is jogging the economic and banking industry. Even when you chat together with your bank's consumer service, there is a superb chance that you are speaking with an AI chatbot. Nevertheless, AI is already poised to change the manner we make investments in economic outlets.

Navigation and Travel

So you possibly have it drilled on your head at this factor that AI infiltrated just about each part of your life. If you think, touring will preserve you safe and unfastened out of your AI overlords, nicely, you're wrong.

Whether you are the usage of Google or Apple Maps, calling up an Uber on your friends, or reserving a flight ticket, AI is proper there assisting you out all the way.

Follow the 10 Steps to Adopt AI in Your Business

One of the things the intelligence industry is in love with is artificial intelligence (AI). Which has different applications which have a different range starting from high-end data science to automated customer service, this technology is covering all across the globe and the enterprise. Let us discuss how your business can benefit safely and efficiently.

Artificial intelligence (AI) is obviously and very clearly a growing force in the modern-day technology industry as it is taking a center position at conferences and showing a huge amount of potential across a wide variety of industries, which includes retail and manufacturing. New products are continuously being embedded with virtual assistants, while chatbots are 24/7 available to answer any of your questions at the supplier's site to your web hosting service provider's support page. Same as, big and advancing companies such as Google, Microsoft, and Salesforce are integrating AI as an intelligence layer across their entire tech stack. Yes, so we can say Al is having Its moment across the world and is ruling the industry.

It's not that the AI that pop culture has changed or made us expect; it's not sentient robots or Skynet, or even Tony Stark's Jarvis assistant. This AI major efflux is happening under the surface Infront of everyone's eyes , which is also making our existing technologies smarter and unlocking the power of all the data that enterprises collect. What exactly does that mean : with the Widespread advancement in machine learning (ML), computer vision, deep learning, and natural language processing (NLP) all these have made it easier as baking a cake to use an algorithm theorem in your work.

For businesses, particularly practical AI applications can be added in all sorts of ways depending on what exactly are needs of your organization, and the business intelligence (BI) get information derived from the data you collect.

Enterprises will use AI for everything from mining social information to driving engagement in client relationship management (CRM) to optimizing supply and potency once it involves chase and managing assets.

ML is taking part in a key role within the development of AI, noted Luke Tang, head of TechCode's world AI+ Accelerator program, that incubates AI startups and helps corporations incorporate AI on prime of their existing merchandise and services.

"Right now, Artificial Intelligence is being driven by all the recent progress in Machine Learning. There is no one single breakthrough that can be pointed to, but the business value we can extract from Machine Learning now is off the charts. " Tang said. "From the point of view of an enterprise, what is happening right now could cause disruption in some core corporate business processes around control and coordination: reporting, scheduling, and resource allocation."

We are providing a few tips from some experts to explain the steps businesses can take to add and use AI in your organization and to make sure that whatever you implement, becomes successful...

1. Get Familiar With AI

Take the time to become at home with what fashionable AI will do. The TechCode Accelerator offers its startups a large array of resources through its partnerships with organizations like university and companies within the AI area. you must conjointly make the most of the wealth of on-line data and resources offered to inform yourself with the fundamental ideas of AI. Tang recommends a number of the remote workshops and on-line courses offered by organizations like Udacity as straightforward ways that to induce started with AI and to extend your data of areas like cubic centimetre and prophetic analytics among your organization.

- Given below are a number of online resources that you can use to get started:

- Intro to AI course and AI Nanodegree Program of Udacity

- Stanford University's online lectures: AI: Principles & Techniques

- AI online course offered through Columbia University on edx

- Microsoft's open-source Cognitive Toolkit helping developers master deep-learning algorithms

- Open-source (OS) of Google Tensor Flow software library for machine intelligence

- AI Resources, AN ASCII text file code directory from the AI Access Foundation

- The Association for the Advancement of computer science (AAAI)'s Resources Page

- MonkeyLearn's light Guide to Machine Learning
- Hawking and Elon Musk's way forward for Life Institute
- OpenAI, AN open trade, and academia-wide deep-learning initiative

2. Not Identify the Problems A person Want AI to Fix

Once you're up to be able to date on the essentials, the next step for almost any business is to get started exploring different ideas. Think about ways to add AJE capabilities for your existing items and services. More significantly, your business should have inside mind specific use circumstances in which AI may solve business problems or perhaps provide demonstrable value.

"When we're working with some sort of company, we start along with an overview of it is key tech programs plus problems. We want to be able to demonstrate how natural vocabulary processing, image recognition, CUBIC CENTIMETERS, and so forth in shape into those products, typically with a workshop involving some type with the supervision of the company, very well Tang explained. "The particulars always vary by business. For example, if typically the company does video CCTV surveillance, it could capture a great deal of value with the addition of CUBIC CENTIMETERS to that process. Inches

3. Prioritize Concrete Worth

Next, you need to be able to assess the potential organization and financial associated using the various possible AJAI implementations you've identified. It can easy to fail to find a way out found in "pie in the sky" AI discussions, but Tang stressed the importance associated with tying your initiatives immediately to business value.

"To prioritize, look at the particular dimensions of potential plus feasibility and put these people into a 2x2 matrix," Tang said. "This should help you prioritize based on the near-term presence and know what typically the financial value is with regard to the company. For this kind of step, you usually require ownership and recognition by managers and top-level professionals. "

4. Acknowledge typically the Internal Capability Space

Discover a stark difference involving what you want to be able to accomplish and what you might have the organizational ability in order to actually achieve within some sort of given period of time. Tang reported a business ought to be able to know what it's in a position of and exactly what it's not from a new tech and business procedure perspective before launching directly into a full-blown AI rendering.

"Sometimes this can require a long time to carry out," Tang said. "Addressing your internal capability distance means identifying what an individual needs to acquire in addition to any processes that will need to be internally progressed before you get proceeding. Depending on the company, there may be current projects or teams of which can help do this particular organically for certain company units. "

5. Deliver in Experts and Place up a Pilot Job

Once your business is usually ready from your company and tech standpoint, next, it's time to acquire and integrate. Tang stated the most important components here are to start out smaller, have project goals inside the mind, and, most significantly, be familiar with what you understand and what you cannot understand about AI. This will be where attracting outside authorities, or AI consultants can easily be invaluable.

"You no longer need a lot regarding moment for a first job; usually for any pilot job, 2-3 months is the good range," Tang said. "You want to be able to bring internal and exterior people together in some sort of team, maybe 4-5 people young and old, and that tighter period frame can keep the group focused on straightforward aims.

After the pilot is completed, you have to be able to decide what the longer-term, more elaborate project will probably be and whether the price proposition makes sense intended for your business. It is essential that expertise from the two sides--the people who understand the business enterprise and typically the people who know concerning AI-- are merged on the pilot project team.

6. Form a Taskforce to Integrate Data

Tang noted that, before employing ML into the business, an individual needs to clean important computer data to make it prepared to avoid a "garbage in, garbage out" situation.

"Internal corporate data is usually typically spread out inside multiple data silos involving different legacy systems, and even may even be inside the hands of various business groups with diverse priorities," Tang explained. "Therefore, a very crucial step toward obtaining premium quality data is to type a cross-[business unit] taskforce, integrate distinct data sets together, plus sort out inconsistencies; therefore that the data is usually accurate and rich, along with all the right measurements required for ML. inch

7. Start Small

Get started applying AI to some sort of small sample of your current data rather than dealing with too much too rapidly. "Start simple, use AJE incrementally to prove worth, collect feedback, and next expand accordingly, " explained Aaron Brauser, Vp associated with Solutions Management at M*Modal, which offers natural terminology understanding (NLU) tech with regard to health care organizations since well as an AJE platform that integrates together with electronic medical records (EMRs).

A specific type associated with data could be data on certain medical expertise. "Be selective about exactly what the AI will become reading," said Doctor. Gilan El Saadawi, Main Medical Information Officer (CMIO) at M*Modal. "For illustration, select a certain problem a person wants to solve, concentrate the AI upon it, plus give it a special question to answer in addition to not throw each of the information at it."

8. To include storage as part of the AI Plan

After you crank up from a little sample of info, you will have to consider the storage area requirements to apply an AI alternative, in accordance with Philip Pokorny, Main Technical Official (CTO) at Penguin Processing, a company that provides high-performance processing (HPC), AI, and ML remedies.

"Improving algorithms is essential to reaching study benefits. But without large volumes of files to help construct more accurate versions, AI methods cannot improve plenty of to accomplish your computing aims," Pokorny composed in a light document entitled, "Critical Judgements: HELPFUL INFORMATION to Building the entire Artificial Intelligence Answer Without Regrets." "That is why the inclusion of quick, optimized storage is highly recommended at the beginning of AI program design."

In addition, you need to optimize AI safe-keeping for information ingest, workflow, and modelling, he advised. "Making the effort to review your alternatives can have an enormous, positive effect on the way the system runs as soon as it is on the web," Pokorny added in.

9. Incorporating Artificial Intelligence as Part of Your Daily Tasks

With the excess information and automation supplied by AI, workers have got a tool to create AI an integral part of their day to day routine rather than a thing that replaces it, in accordance with Dominic Wellington, Global It again Evangelist at Moogsoft, a service provider of AI for this functions (AIOps). "Some personnel may be cautious with technology that may affect their employment, so introducing the perfect solution is in an effort to augment their everyday tasks is essential," Wellington discussed.

He added that companies ought to be transparent on what the tech performs to resolve concerns in the workflow. "Thus giving staff members an 'under the hood' knowledge in order to clearly imagine how AI augments their purpose rather than eradicating it," he stated.

10. Build With Balance

When you're developing an AI method, it requires a variety of meeting the requirements of the technology along with the research study, Pokorny discussed. "The overarching concern, even prior to starting to create an AI program, is that you ought to build the machine with stability," Pokorny mentioned. "This might sound evident but, all too often, AI systems were created around specific areas of how the crew envisions obtaining its research objectives, without understanding certain requirements and limitations on the hardware and program that would assist the research. The effect is really a less-than-optimal, also a dysfunctional program that does not achieve the required goals."

To do this balance, companies have to build in ample bandwidth for storage space, the graphics running device (GPU), and networking. Safety measures can be an oft-overlooked component aswell. AI, by its mother nature, requires the usage of wide swaths of info to accomplish its job.

Ensure that you understand what forms of data will undoubtedly be associated with the job and your usual safety measures safeguards -- encryption, electronic private sites (VPN), and anti-malware -- may possibly not be enough.

"Similarly, you must balance the way the overall budget can be spent to accomplish research with the necessity to protect against energy failure along with other situations through redundancies," Pokorny mentioned. "You may even need to make in flexibility to permit repurposing of equipment as user specifications change."

How is AI impacting everyday life?

Automated Transport System

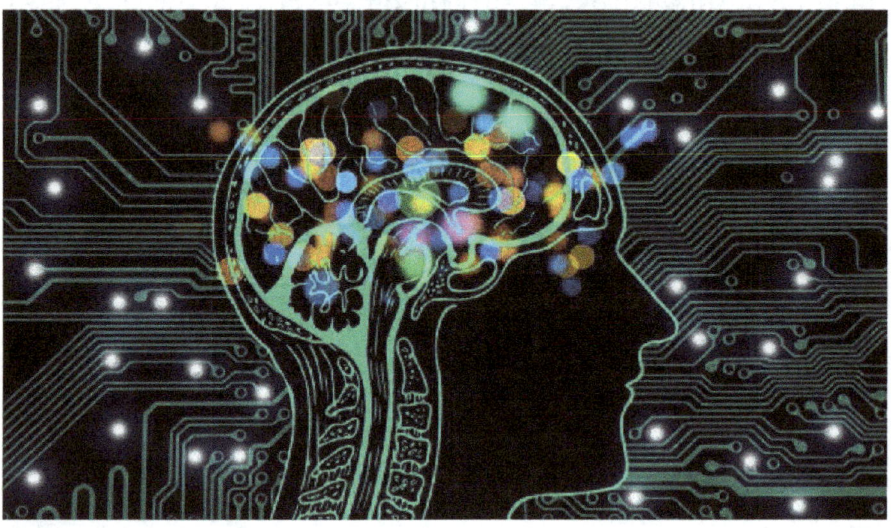

The transport marketplace has considerably embraced improvement in technology. In accordance with (Zhang and Minbiole 2016), folks have implemented AI engineering to build up self-driving cars. Even though the cars require a driver for protection purposes, the innovations are obvious proof of the amount of AI so far as technological advancements are worried. For instance, creating a car step itself and around sides is hard. The technology that allows the same auto to get around crossroads and prevent colliding with different vehicles is critically innovative (Cunha et al. 2016). Just as making each one of these things happen is definitely magical, and lots of skills and understanding is borrowed through the AI. AI because the technologies behind self-driving automobiles have improved individuals' everyday activity in several techniques. Through self-driving, the number of accidents occurring features substantially decreased (Harper, Hendrickson and Samaras 2016). Generally, accidents are related to several factors such as liquor, over speeding, prescription drugs, aggressive driving, insufficient encounter, ignorance of highway signs plus the set conditions, constant reaction moment and overcompensation.

Considering that about 40% of complete accidents occur because of the influence of alcoholic beverages and substance abuse. Consequently, a lot more than 1100 lives happen to be lost that could be preserved through the full execution of self-driven automobiles.

INVOLVEMENT IN DANGEROUS JOBS

AI produced robots are increasingly being designed to support humans in taking hazardous circumstances. Robots took over positions that are hazardous to humans (Smith & Anderson 2014). A number of dangerous jobs incorporate defusing bombs, which create plenty of risk to a real human. Therefore, along with the advancement of robots, diffusing bombs have grown to be easy because the robots can perform it easily with little or nothing to fear. Because of this, robots have substantially assisted in keeping thousands of lifetime in overtaking the most hazardous job in depends upon right now (Abdalla et al. 2016). Finally, with more improvements in AI, extra positions will undoubtedly be bought out by robots, which might consist of welding which generates some toxins. People operating under intense temperature and within an atmosphere with earsplitting noises will significantly take advantage of the understanding of AI. In this respect, the execution of AI possesses helped considerably to provide safety precautions to humans and offer protection from injury (Helbing et al. 2017).

COMPUTERIZED METHODS

In accordance with Vermesan and his fellow workers (2017), nowadays, automated methods of reason, understanding, and just how people perceive have grown to be a section of people's day to day activities. Through the use of GPS through the long drives and travels, the usage of smartphone technology will be good examples in the role AI has got performed in people's life. With AI, there's been the minimal event of errors, particularly when typing because the computers can forecast what we will write and produce corrections to wrongly typed phrases. That is clearly a clear exemplary case of an AI device at work. In addition, whenever folks are uploading images on social web sites, the AI algorithm recognizes the individual and tags them (Smith & Eckroth 2017). On top of that, the data of AI is usually well employed in the bank and finance institutions to control and arrange statistical data consequently. The usage of AI technology possesses reduced the number of errors and raising the probability of achieving accuracy.

Additionally, AI features significantly contributed in neuro-scientific medical analysis and analysis of sophisticated neurological disorders. For example, while using AI, medical doctors can determine a patient's health threats and determine the medial side effects of numerous medications (Hussain and Qamar 2016).

Exclusively, AI has inspired the industry of medical analysis leading to state-of-the-art study which has, in turn, resulted in saving lives.

Evidently, a lot of the people understand the significance of AI, as well as the role it offers played in boosting their lives. From the chart previously mentioned, 59% of individuals decided that AI acquired greatly affected their lifetime, 24% didn't recognize the position enjoyed by AI and 17% didn't find out whether it acquired played any element or not.

REDUCED HUMAN EFFORT

AI has enjoyed an essential purpose in daily human beings' life. Today, several industries are employing human technology within the development of equipment that performs real human pursuits (Frey and Osborne 2017). These resources create consistency inside the rate of manufacturing with performance and effectiveness, guaranteeing the supervision of quality jobs. Therefore, the launch of AI technologies in every facet of life, promises of the error-free world. It really is so since devices can work regularly without exhausting, unlike humans, accelerating the functions of carrying out the tasks and will be offering accurate results.

It really is clear that AI has taken about increased development in production establishments because of its ability to conduct different functions (Brynjolfsson & McAfee 2014). On top of that, AI can be used in companies in general management systems where they're used to help keep employees' records, draw out data that allows in decision planning. Majorly, the part of AI has got enabled control and production market sectors to perform their jobs in a good moment and enhance organization development.

TIME-SAVING

Time will be of great substance nowadays, and people are prepared to develop devices that assist in saving time. In accordance with Gurkaynak and his acquaintances (2016), AI features proven to conserve time and properly increase every second. It can perform several jobs at a chance efficiently with a higher swiftness compared to people. Similarly, they are able to collect data and provide solutions to the issues through the evaluation of exactly the same data considerably faster than individuals (Brynjolfsson & McAfee 2014). Apparently, the AI systems can do to date more than people can do. Furthermore, with AI, recurring tasks have already been eliminated, which human beings spend enough time trying to get rid of. Through AI, staff no longer focus on repetitive tasks but rather concentrate on more difficult concerns (Makridakis 2017). So, AI has taken about changes that have significantly increased in our day to day lives.

Artificial Intelligence Impacting

Teaching, Learning, & Education

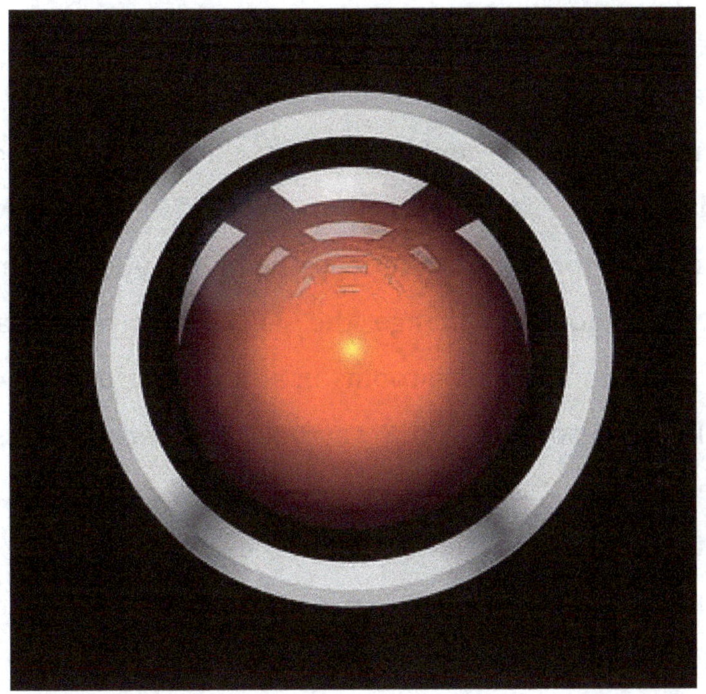

It is an open secret that all human actions are based on anticipations, but we somehow cannot predict the future because we do not have data for it as it has not yet happened. However, we can definitely use our current life experience and knowledge to imagine how tomorrow will be and drive things in that direction. If we are able to understand the past that has given rise to the present, we might also be able to have a good insight into the future. Now in order to understand the opportunities that AI could bring, we first need to understand AI in the current world and what could the society be like when AI is widely used in the future. AI has the ability to change the way things have been happening. For example, it can change the structure of teaching and education in so many different ways that it could pose new challenges to academia and education too. Ai could amplify skill differences as well as equalize the opportunities for learning to everyone around the world. It could also change the concept of how learning happens. It can bring classrooms in a new form or may delete them. It may also change the way teachers teach in classes or may require the students to adopt a very different approach to learning based on the foundations of the technology.

It could also play a big role in the democratization of power and may put an end to monopolies. It could give rise to income equality and put an end to global poverty too. And this all is possible without a doubt, but we need to work over it smart and hard. Now is the best time to do that and is the best time to see and make the outcomes possible of AI. There is a huge buzz in the market around AI these days, and since the area is a bit tough, the hard work is definitely worth it.

AI has been on the top of the policymaking agenda of the US policymakers after 2013 when the brilliant minds like Frey and Osborne predicted that almost half of the jobs in the US would be replaced due to structural changes in the system. This study was further proved correct by researchers in the industries who had also concluded that huge changes and transformations are going to take place in the labor market. At the same time, people with expertise in AI have been offered lucrative jobs in industries and there has been a crazy buzz around AL in the market as well as in academia. The chain claims to be the leader in AI and that they will grow a 150 billion dollar in AI till 2030. Only in 2017, the US department of defence used a huge 2 billion dollars in AI, and the overall private investment in the field is more than 20 billion dollars. Even the AI startups in the EU plans to invest more than 20 billion euros by 202 in the AI.

In small tasks, AI has already exceeded human intelligence. In 2018, a researcher in Stanford developed the Ai system for only one year, and it was able to detect more than 144 types of disease or medical conditions by using frontal view X-ray images, thereby outshining the human diagnostic accuracy of Pneumonia. A very interesting thing happened in 2017 when AlphaGo defeated the world champion in the game of chess. An artificial neural network called AlphaZero achieved a superhuman mental ability in just 24 hours of training and defeated the three-times world champion in the game. Google's CEO Sundar Pichai, stunned people in 2018 when he in his keynote, demonstrated that Duplex-which is an AI system-and which organizes and tackles the appointment system, has been fooling humans that they have been talking to humans and it was AI. So in a society full of AI systems like autonomous cars, robots taking over industries and flood of AI miracles, we cannot deny the fact that AI is becoming the immensely intelligent and with intelligence, comes power too. So AI could avail all the evil and good powers given to in the cultures.

However, the present AI systems are immensely restricted and boundaries have been set for what they can do. They just cannot do whatever they like/want to do. However, an author recently noticed that all the hype around ideas based on AI and that have been discussed over the media are three decades old and that AI could do far more than what is being discussed.

However, there are challenges to the currently dominated models as well. One such challenge to the current dominant learning model is that they only see the world as a repetition of the past and not anticipation or expectation of the future. The learning criteria and the dated and material are supplied or provided by humans. We will present a three-stage learning model that will show that norms and values are also oftentimes, expressed by means of unarticulated, and tacit emotional reactions. Even the most recent and advanced model of learning is also based on the oldest t approach to AL and around all the data and intelligence comes from humans.

However, immense hard work in needed to make the dream of a great future come true. For example, the storing of electricity in electrodes or the arrival of Edison electric did not start the electric revolution. It took huge time and the impact and transformation of the general-purpose became a reality after a long time when economies and societies reinvent themselves as users of the latest technology. However, technological changes require cultural changes too, and this is reflected in policies, lifestyles, social institutions, norms, education, as well as skill sets. As a result of this all, AI-now called new electricity-might brings a revolution in many areas when it gets a huge user base despite the fact that it is self-driven too.

This will lead to the birth of new things out of the old running systems and the reinvention of knowledge creation, learning and its applications in many industries and research centres. It will, in the end, give rise to a whole different and new social and cultural system with new ways of learning and teaching and making things happen.

Let's focus on some questions that address the relevance of and shift in the structure of educational places and the change in policies. Which jobs will come into the market, and which jobs will be deleted?

So what could be the skills that are required in this 21st century where AI is so widely used? How could we include AI in the university curriculum, and how could we use AI to change the way teachers teach? Do we still need to monitor students in the classrooms? Can we use AI to access students without any biasness? Do we need any building to have classrooms in or there is no need for classrooms? Is Ai able to overcome the ill effects of diseases such as dyslexia or other learning disabilities? These are some of the most asked questions but answering them is not a piece of cake and requires immense research.

The aim of this very report is to out such questions into context to address them in a meaningful way possible. We would also be focusing on the background discussion that will provide hints for discussion and will lead us to some final arguments or answers that are needed to make the society the best place and favorable to use the applications of AI. In order to this tedious task, we need to dissect AI-first and see what is inside. So this should be very clear that there are so many things that AI could do very well and there are things that AI can never do or may be possible in future but not present. Currently, there is a huge buzz in the market and is however not very easy to recognize the best questions out of a plethora of them. However, in order to have a realistic future, it is very important to have a good understanding of the basic principles of AI, the context in which it is applied in learning, education and teaching and then focuses on some specific forms of AI that is adaptive neural network which is responsible for the recent rising interest in AI.

A three-level model of action to analyses Artificial Intelligence and its impact

There have been three hierarchically attached to human behavior as distinguished by the cultural-historical theory of activity. First of all, behavior could be analyzed as a social and meaningful work directed and controlled by socially and culturally constructed motives. Through goal-oriented acts, activities could be realized and could lead to problem-solving after that. Then using the tools available, operations could be implemented in the current situation and concrete context. There is however a very important aspect to this three-level hierarchy and that is that we cannot reduce the levels to each other. The meaning of any activity could be explained using cultural, social and historical terms that normally do not make sense at the operation level. For instance, we could explain both object and purpose by putting it in the sense that we are teaching to give rise to responsible citizen and individuals, well-paid jobs, and so on.

The output of the activity mentioned above, however, could be decoded into solid acts which further depends on factors like norms, social principles, institutions, the social division of labor and the ways and procedures in which societies organizes social production and many other factors. These social factors shape and give structure to our activities. These also give rise to an implicit normative, anticipatory and emotional background which gives foundation to the running system to go on. This level also gives the foundation to ethics of actions.

The link and correlation between activity and act are thereby similar to the link between utterances and words. Words are needed for utterance as well as for acts for activity expression. However, understanding the meaning of the utterance is also difficult if the words are not defined. In order to write a statement, we need words and for words, we definitely need letters but it is not possible to comprehend the meaning of sentences just by understanding the meaning of letters and words. This means that it is not possible to build a model of human behavior just by understanding the meaning of words and letters. For a proper understanding of activities, social and inter-generational learning is important and human activity level could not be accessed just by the empirical testing of human behavior.

The level of an act, on the other hand, contains internally and externally observable behavior. In addition, the activity level answer a culturally, socially and historical and meaningful question "why" and the question of "WHY" is answered by the level of acts. Teaching description on this level could be, for instance, "I am writing this book". The third and last operational level focuses on the question "how" setting could be implemented in concrete settings. For example, there could be a plethora of ways for assessing and examining students' skills and many types of homework and ways to deliver it to students. This is the level of technology operation as a tool and this level could be let's say that "I am attaching a picture to a slide". Learning theorists and psychologists have been focusing on many levels of the three-level hierarchy since the last century. Associationist and behaviouristic theories of learning have mainly addressed the operation levels. In addition, constructivist and cognitivist learning theories have focused mainly on cognitive levels, and constructionists are also focusing on the material and social context. Theorists, who are socio culturists, have been often focusing on cultural, social and material learning. In figure 1, some famous theorists have been depicted these three levels.

A human can learn on all the three-level of activity of the hierarchy. When our habits or routines are restricted by any obstacle, our operational response gets replaced by actions. In such cases, we try to interpret the problem in question and quest for a possible solution. At this very level, learning is all about problem-solving which also lead to the formation of new models too. New ways and procedure of dealing with problems appear and could be internalized and adopted. Lev Vygotsky was the founder of cultural-historical theory and he had also focused and put emphasis on the important role of cultural and social activities that modify human thinking and learning. The birth of new and more advanced forms of thought is made possible for they also rely upon historically and culturally developed knowledge. So it is very obvious that cognitive level activities make use of resources both from the top level and bottom level operations. Vygotsky also focused on the impact of cultural and social factors on cognitive development. Engeström has also elucidated the role of learning and its importance in the creation of new educational practices and activities.

In a conceptual frame like this one, learning the activity level could be easily understood as a realization and innovation of imagined features.

Opportunities and possibilities that are normally figured out or discovered at cognition level could turn social practices and activity systems upside down thereby giving rise to space for more but new motives and purpose to begin with social organization. However, most of this development as a result of activities is unintended and self-emergent. Complies social interactions give rise to and shape social institutions, structures and practices. This, however, remains unidentified to a large number of society members.

The three-level models enable us to start with an easy and useful foundation to understand AU and the possible impacts it could have on human life and activities. The entry of AI into social practices and operations gives rise to the efficiency of work and increase the marginal productivity of labor and machines. It also automates and replaces as well as substitutes humans in jobs previously been held by humans. So when AI enters social practices, it changes and transforms the motive system and outdate current specializations and activities. For instance, routine and technical skills emphasis the operational level. In addition, vocational training has also focused on this skill set of teaching how to make use of domain-specific knowledge and use the underlying tools.

The recent system of education is more focused on problem-solving, and I think it gives rise to scholars and critical thinkers who have the decision making abilities and entrepreneurial competence to make things happen and create values out of scratch. I think have a skill set that modern 21st-century need is crucial as it addresses opportunities for cultural and social changes that take place at activity levels.

At the same time, learning at the operation level needs data on the present concrete environment. Normally data for such operations could be generated by using physical interactions and perception. At the level of socially motivated activity, learning, on the other hand, needs knowledge basic knowledge about social systems of meaning. In order to absorb such knowledge, communication language, as well as dialogue, becomes imperative. Technology is a very important factor and indicates a change in the current system. Technology in the current industrialized era focuses on making tools for innovation and growth. So all three levels of activity have somehow complex dependencies. This model is also currently been inspected in the interaction between child and robot (social robotics). We will be focusing briefly on the three different kinds of AI and to locate their abilities in this hierarchy as well as to discuss the potential of the three kinds of AI.

So to talk about modern lives, we may fractal structure. This three-level model of activity elucidates that many different kinds of AI and machine learning systems work on different layers of hierarchy. The level of meaningful activity is fundamental according to the sociocultural theory of learning and throw light on an advanced form of human learning and intelligence, which is outside the current scope of AI.

Three types of AI

Historically, AI could be categorized into three alternate approaches: they are

- Data based
- Knowledge-based and
- Logic-based

The first of the list that is data-based is also termed as machine learning and artificial neural networks. However, it is surprising that the recent innovations and success in AI also depict the old approaches to AI.

Data-based neural AI

It was Nicolas Rashevsky, who first of all developed certain mathematical models for neural networks as early as the

1930s. The models made news only when his student Pitts elucidated biological neural networks in 1942 and termed it as networks of logical switches.

Pitts and Warren published the paper, and the publication took place after Alan Turing had written about the mechanization of formal logic which led to the appearance of the first digital computer. With this, it became evident that all the formal logical sequences could be simulated and mechanized by such neural networks. The brain was viewed as a computer and computer was termed as the electric brain. The metaphor became part of English literature and has been widely quoted since then. The two-lined metaphor has in it, a whole discussion about research in organizational and cognitive sciences and now influences the connectivity model of learning, economics and many areas of popular and scientific thinking.

Neural network models informed by neurobiology has provided a foundation for the present neural artificial intelligence. The most important and earliest contribution was made by **Frank Rosenblatt** in the 1950s. He was inspired by the famous neuropsychologist's stance that learning takes place in the neural networks by the process of synaptic modification and by the famous economist **Friedrich Hayek** who worked on distributed learning. So Frank suggested that learning in the biological neural networks could be pictured as a slow change in the network connection. Frank presented a multi-layered picture of his findings, which in many ways, is similar to the current advanced neural networks.

It, however, is different from today's AI system in that modern systems are laden with numerous deep-learning and neural-learning systems and the process is done by using machines which are billion times faster than the one (IBM 704) Frank used for his research and findings.

The simple behavioristic learning model of most of the AI is the only single feature that differentiates them. Others include the presence of very advanced computational needs and the need for data during learning. For such systems, the presence of data is the most important success factor, and if data is not there, there is no success. If we use biological terminology for such a thing, we would call it "Datavores." It is due to this very reason that we call this "Data-based" approach to AI.

Logic- and knowledge-based AI

Neural Network models (NNMs) had been pretty popular in the 1950s and 60s too. These models were also considered as a key to studying language, abstraction and creativity in the Dartmouth summer research projects back in 1956, where the term artificial intelligence was coined. Despite continued work on neural networks, research in artificial intelligence swiftly shifted to "symbolic processing."

According to the famous mathematicians after Hilbert and Russell, logical truth could be extracted or derived from the formal sentence manipulation. And this is an open secret that the computer cannot and was not able to make the logical inference back then. Another commendable effort was made by Logic Theorist which was put forward by Allen Newell, Herbert Simon and John Shaw over the snowy Christmas break back in 1955. This was the solution to the problem and the system could not break the logical structure and could manipulate it very well. It additionally could derive proof of logical theories. All three researchers were sure they had created a mechanical brain that could think. This was soon followed by General

Problem Solver that could solve just any logical problem that made sense and had a solution.

The dominant approach to AI had been the logical approach from 1950 to the 1970s. By the late 1970s, it was however though and accepted that human thinking could not be explained and simulated just be a mere explanation of logical statements. As a result, the central focus of AI became domain-specific knowledge. This also gave rise to an "expert system" or more specifically, knowledge-based systems. An early example of this was the SHRDLU natural language understanding program and the MYCIN medical diagnostic system, which was widely used for recommendation of medicine and dosage based on symptoms of the disease.

It had a very general interface engine and a domain-specific knowledge based on human intelligence.

In expert systems, in particular, domain knowledge try to copy and pretend human expert knowledge structure. In the 1980s, the expert systems had made huge news and way well known with around 2/3 of the Fortune 500 companies using the system on a daily basis. As they have been in wide use in different sectors in the economy, for instance, financial system, logistic system, manufacturing system and logistics as well as automation of business processes. Since the early 1980s, a number of expert systems have been made for education and learning. The trend of knowledge-based artificial intelligence diminished towards the end of the decade as it was, by then, evident that the development of domain-specific knowledge bases needed expert knowledge engineers and also due to the spread of internet and computer which shifted the interest towards automation of business processes and system integration. These days, the standard programming environments make use of many ideas of stand-alone expert systems. However, as the rise of knowledge-based artificial intelligence declined slowly, there was a rise in the neural Ai for a few years.

There is, however, bottlenecks in the system integrations and parallel programming too. These difficulties have restricted AI systems to universities and laboratories only. As a result, the attention got focused on mobile internet and world-wide-web as the new trends. In practice, both knowledge-based and logic-based approached in Ai focuses on the cognitive level of activity hierarchy. Cognition was also interpreted in a purely individualistic way. AI has been helpful in designing general algorithms for thinking which manipulates symbols, as humans do-the argument. While logic-based systems have been focusing on the solving process of general problems. Knowledge-based approach, on the other hand, made use of simple models of inference and a more elucidated interpretation of domain-specific knowledge, the argument being that effective decision making needs more knowledge and not logic.

In contrast, ML (machine learning) and ANN (artificial neural network) typically make use of learning models that could be characterized as behavioristic. The systems have normally a pre-defined criterion which gives detail about optimal response and are also provided with a huge amount of data. Algorithms do not copy or imitating human intelligence in such systems.

Instead, they make use of the training data practices and define strategies for adapting the output of the system. In applications like games, the training data could automatically be generated; however, in the most recent and important neural network; humans provide data. A good example is the arrival of the best of the best image recognition AI system. To a large extent, AI systems rely on a public ImageNet database that has around 14 million images. Using the Amazon Mechanical Truck crowdsourcing platform, the labelling of objects in the image was done.

Recent & future developments in AI

The current interest in AI is the result of three development that took place at the same time. The first and foremost is the high interest in realistic computer games that need special graphic processors. Fast parallel programming became available at a low cost when the PC graphic card making company Nvidia launched its CUDA programming interface. Its graphics accelerator card was known around the world. This also gave researchers a chance to make neural networks with many interconnected layers made out of artificial neurons with a big number of the parameter for the network to learn. Secondly, a huge amount of data became available as computers and users got linked. This digitalization of video, image, text and voice has engendered a platform for machine learning to thrive.

This has also given AI researchers the freedom to work on the old artificial neural network models, and a huge data source for training. These data sets have proved to be enough and abundant to tackle some pressing challenges in AI, which also include recognition of objects from digital image and machine translation. Earlier it was also believed that computers also need to know the language as well as the structure so that they could be able to translate the text as well as speech to different languages. For many users, it is enough to just process millions of available sentences to understand the context in which words appear.

Another common way is to make use of publically available GloVe word representations, which have been produced using text corpora that included as much as 840 billion word tokens which are found on documents. And other pages on the internet, and afterward translated to the vocabulary of as much as 2 million words. Using a machine-learning algorithm and these available data set, the world has been plotted in points in 300-dimensional vector space. The geometric relation and location among words in such space capture many features of word use, which could also be used as a foundation for translation from one to another language. Though a pure data-based and statistical approach are not enough to comprehend creative or new uses of languages, and it also works great in practical use.

Thirdly, the testing and creation of the neural network are made easy by specialized open-source ML programming environments. In the latest AI neural systems, learning takes place by slow adjustment of weights of the network. It is further based on if the networks make precise predictions with data training. The basic task in such learning is to provide information about the importance of each neuron's activity. It also provides information about the right and wrong predictions made by neurons. So when there is an association between active neuron and wrong decision, the activity of neurons dwindles as well as the weights of the incoming links and connections. Since there could be several layers of neurons and a number of connections between neurons, this makes the task difficult for even quantum computers. The influence of a neuron over a prediction could also be assessed by using chain rule in calculus, which shows the propagation of information from the outer layer of the network, layer by layer to the inner layer. This is termed as "backpropagation" of error. And yes, the calculation and computation of network making use of this model might involve a billion of computations in the advanced networks. Latest neural artificial intelligence development platforms can easily get it done with a couple of lines of program coding.

These trends started getting together in 2012 when a multi-trained network trained with the leading Nvidia's graphic cards showed an outstanding performance in image recognition competition. The competition was actually based on a database of ImageNet that included around 14 million images annotated by humans. ILSVRC (ImageNet Large Scale Visual Recognition Challenge) is now the leading benchmark for the success of artificial intelligence. Along with the other 100 objects, the classification challenge and object detection of the object makes use of around 1.2 million images for training. In 2017, the best

NN architectures had been able to guess the exact object category with 97.7% precision and top 5% accuracy. This meant that the correct object in question was among the five most probable classes as projected by the network. The instant improvement in object recognition that gives top-5 rates of errors for the winner over the years.

The revival of neural artificial intelligence has, in part, been caused by the provision of detailed electronic texts, digital images, social work linkages and internet search patterns. The recent advancement has also been accelerated by the fact that such huge data sets are not easy to utilize and analyze with the common computer. ML requires big data, but it has the ability to make such big data useful and valuable. This is why ML is so extensively used in industries because there is a huge number of commercial profits and incentives as a result of using such models which is not possible for the ordinary computer.

Models of learning in data-based Artificial Intelligence

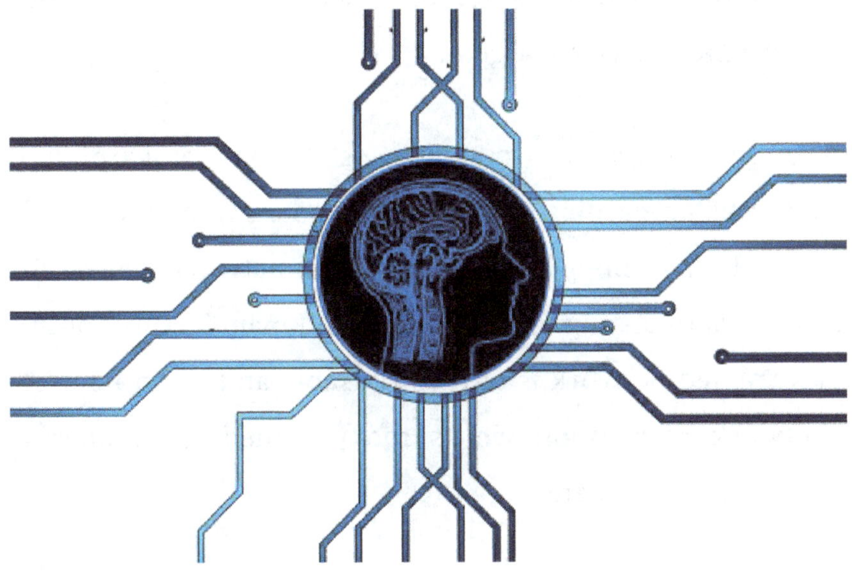

All the latest AI systems are based on something called a supervised model of learning. It is the training data that provide the foundation for a supervised model of learning. Training data is provided by human, and it is advantageous because it enables us to adjust the network weights when labels of training data are incorrectly predicted. After providing a good number of examples, the errors could be reduced and decreased to a certain level at which predictions ate useful for practical purposes. For instance, if an image program tries to distinguish between cows and goats, then during the training process, someone needs to give input to the system if a pic has a cow or goat.

Another good alternative to a supervised model of learning is termed transfer learning. We know that a large amount of data is required for training a complete neural network which will make it learn to distinguish important and main features of the data. A trained network is always reusable and could be used for network recognition works too provided the underpin features are all complete.

For instance, a network could be trained to recognize human faces by with a million images in data. Once the system is able to recognize each face that was used as data for training the deep layers of the system gets optimized for face recognition. The system could then be trained to detect a new face that was not used in the data and had never been seen before. This waives off the requirement for computation and data to a huge amount. This means that AI developers do not need to train the system always and could buy trained systems from special vendors dealing with this business. The GloVe vectors, for instance, that has been developed by Stanford University has been used as a starting point for Google's pre-trained inception and for neural language processing. This means that a supervised learning system presumes that we have prior knowledge about the categories input patterns can represent.

This learning model has been used most frequently in artificial intelligence, and due to practical purposes, it is also often enough to categorized patterns into sets of pre-defined classes. An autonomous car should be able to distinguish between a car, a truck, a cyclist and a kid. This is done by supervised learning that gives rise to patterns that are collections of data or input. The intelligence and thinking are this the same as that of a living being and because the learned behavior is associated with environmental conditions.

Since these learning behaviors are explained in the context of Skinnerian reinforcement learning and the Pavlovian theory of reflexes.

As pointed out by **Vygotsky in** 1920, this kind of learning simply represents a developmental model of learning that both birds and humans are equally capable of. One of the challenges for a supervised learning system is that it is not able to see the world in the present and could only do so in the past through data. This means they view the world as a repetition of the past. This is also been reported that the data that is available for training is provided by human records. Cultural and personal biases are thus not inborn but inherent in AI systems based on the use of supervised learning. The model presented above shows the values and norms of tacit and have been expressed in the form of an unarticulated emotional reaction. So it could be said that supervised learning models intertwined and materializes the beliefs of a culture that otherwise often stay unexplored. In a provoking way, supervised learning systems give rise to machines that could only perceive the environment in which humans are pre-defined. From pedagogic and ethical viewpoints, it is not considered good due to their interaction with other AI systems which makes them powerful enough to do things they like which could be dangerous in the long run as debates are hot over it.

Since the 1960s, many supervised models have been developed and employed, and as a result, researchers now have better access to information around the world due to better computational powers. For instance, the AlphaZero game of Google uses an artificial intelligence reinforcement learning system which is very able to give rise to the simulation of games and adjust weights based on game success. The reinforcement learning model is inspired by the Skinnerian model and amplifies behavior in a way that leads to positive outcomes.

A modified form of reinforcement model is a generative adversarial network, also called GANs, and this is interesting as one network tries to fool another and shows that the data it generates is from a training set of data. With this approach, synthetic images of artwork have been created as well as human faces in a way that a machine cannot differentiate between the real human face and the image. Commercially, it has also been used for designing products more widely in the fashion industry. Turing learning is another modified form of GAN, in which the system is allowed to interact actively with people around after learning. It tries to guess the origin of the data.

Towards the future

Ascertain economists, theorists, and experts have complete high-profile declarations about the inevitable appearance of superintelligent AI systems that finally may substitute human being in numerous areas of life, and it is maybe valuable to footnote that most presents AI learning models embody cognitive competencies that most carefully look like biological characters.

Several forecasts about the future of artificial intelligence have remained grounded on extrapolations of past technical progress and in specific guesses of the continuation of "Moore's Law" in calculating, with a slight worry about dissimilarities between innovative forms of human learning and the additional elementary abilities of relationship.

Human learning needs several meta-level capabilities. In specific, for humans, it is essential to know what sums as knowledge, how to go on in obtaining, producing and acquiring knowledge. How to control reasoning, courtesy and sentiment in the process of learning, and what are the communal and applied incentive for learning. As Luckin has freshly pointed out, at present-day AI wants most of the meta-cognitive and controlling competences. It is significant to annotate that the future of the present AI will bang to a significant extent that would be dogged by growths in chip design.

For nearly fifty years, growth in computer and memory chips remained compelled by fast unbroken developments in the reduction of component structures on semiconductor chips. Throughout the last decade, it has become progressively recognized that this expansion is near to end, and new methods are wanted to have the semiconductor industry developing. Neural Artificial Intelligence sermons the "post-Moore" age by shifting growth to new computing models, as well as analogue computing. This signifies a key gap in the technological basics of knowledge foundation. In practice, most Artificial Intelligence specialists toil with "narrow AI," in comparison to "general AI," which would have abilities alike to humans. In the first Dartmouth summer project on AI, the chief investigators said that computers would soon be intelligent. Such hopes appear to be impractical even today. Though it may be likely to grow AI structures that have abilities that closely look like human intellect, present AI systems custom somewhat basic models of learning as well as biological intelligence.

Many present-day AI systems depend on fundamentally reflexological and behaviouristic learning models, promoted by scientists Pavlov and Thorndike at the start of the 20th century. So they might also better be termed as mechanical predispositions, in place of AI. In spite of these limits, the power of Artificial Intelligence in education has been extensively acknowledged throughout the past three decades. Though the influence on schoolrooms has been comparatively slight, the new developments propose that the condition might shift. In specific, AI-based systems can develop extensive use as systems that backs teachers and beginners. AI could also quickly adjust the economy and labor market, generating new necessities for education and educational systems.

Impacts of AI on Skill & Competence demand

One of the important roles of the present educational system is that it makes capabilities that permit people to contribute to the economic domain of life. The past of educational systems is thoroughly related to the growth of the industrial society, and wage labor is still a dominant establishing code in industrial societies. In advanced policy debates, education is consequently presumed as a cause of employment. Education, in such understanding, is a crucial motorist of economic yield and effectiveness, and policies around education are outlined in the perspective of economic development. So it is significant to inquire also from the standpoint of educational systems how AI would alter jobs and labor markets. For economists, the primary query has been if mechanization and automation upsurge unemployment. As technologies upturn labor productivity, fewer human labors are wanted to uphold production. If the demand for goods raises enough, joblessness grows. In actuality, this meek model is, no doubt, too simple. If technologies substitute specific jobs, folks night transfer to others. Over-all, this is what occurred last century when agrarian and manufacturing jobs were computerized, and workers switched to services.

Many influential studies have confirmed this design. Using past statistics, they characteristically accomplish that additional skill and labor output have not augmented cumulative unemployment.

In contrast, it is well-known that a significant cause why mechanization has not produced tenacious joblessness is population rise that has unceasingly amplified demand for manufacturing goods and services. Numerous other causes, such as globalization, education, amplified ingesting of non-recyclable natural capitals, also, growths in healthcare, science have been involved in the 20th-century economic development, and is, therefore, hard to create forecasts about the future by making use of traditional designs. Though some powerful readings claim that mechanization has not produced joblessness, it may consequently be valuable to recall also the past of mechanization and its social concerns. Industrialization directed to communicative disorders and revolts from Prussia to Mexico, Russia, and states around the globe, often with vicious products.

Lots of lives were mislaid. Societies gathered into metropolises, and at the crack of the 20th-century writers like Jack London still labeled in part the miserable circumstances of wage-slaves in the Oakland harbors. As the economic system currently works on a global scale, the influence of AI could not effortlessly be calculated on a national scale, where valuable econometric statistics characteristically is accessible.

Though country-level statistics can be combined, for instance, for cross-national assessments, the worldwide and schmoosed knowledge economy is not just a group of economically unified national economies. In seeing the communal, economic and human influence of AI and its link with educational policies, a comprehensive opinion on social transformation is necessary.

AI impact of Skills in economic studies

Most of the contemporary economic reading on the prospect of work in the future and the influence of Artificial intelligence begins with observing the effect of computers on talent demand. It is, consequently, crucial to comprehend how talents and work jobs have gotten inferred in these readings. Underneath, we situate these econometric readings from the perspective of the three-level model explained above (see 2.1), displaying that diverse kinds of AI have abilities on distinct stages of the model. Most of the persuasive econometric readings make use of the U.S. Occupational Information.

Network (OINET) catalog as an initial point. OINET covers now about 1000 work-related descriptions to aid job seekers, students, and educators to comprehend ability wants and toil content in diverse occupations.

The ground-breaking research by Frey and Osborne enquired specialists in AI and robotics what are those possible holdups that prevent the mechanization of labor work. Using these computerization blockages as an initial point, they then enquired the specialists to categorize a set of OINET jobs grounded on whether mechanization of their jobs seemed conceivable. Those jobs that didn't encompass hard-to-automate tasks remained categorized as having a significant risk of being automated. A critical upshot of the Frey and Osborne reading is that it foretold that about partial of U.S. jobs are at great peril of being mechanized shortly using present-day technologies. Whether this approximation is precise or not, it still elaborates the opinion that educational systems will be below strong gravity to discourse this wide-spread change. The outdated educational arrangement has vexed to forecast the future demand for diverse kinds of education founded on projected labor market growths. Frey and Osborne displayed that AI will have an essential influence on the labor market, and generate breaks in numerous trends that presently reinforce educational development and policies. We, consequently, need to reassess both the content and the purposes of education in this fresh setting.

AI impacts on Skill-biased and task-biased models of technology

Many previous studies on the impact of computers and automation were based on skill-biased prototypes of the technological amendment. In skill-biased models, occupations that do not need cultured, knowledgeable, and skillful labors are vulnerable to mechanization. In such models, PCs are projected to be used mostly for jobs that need narrow skills. It is natural to undertake that to circumvent joblessness people need extra and higher-level education as well as training.

On the other hand, current studies on mechanization have accepted a task-biased method. It accepts that those jobs that can be precisely defined can be programmed with a computer. In these lessons, jobs that entail tedious tasks are vulnerable to mechanization. This has characteristically directed investigators to assume that jobs that need human-like intellect are not vulnerable to computerization. The effect for educational policy could be that education should emphasis on non-routine mental tasks, often branded as 21st-century expertise. Osborne and Frey used a task-biased model, but they reasoned for a diverse tactic. In their opinion, the effect on AI and automation must be studied grounded on present technological tailbacks. AI is quickly becoming able to achieve tasks that have conventionally been agreed upon to need human thought.

According to Frey and Osborne, it is consequently significant to ask specialists what computers cannot ensure. All those errands where practical blocks do not occur may be computerized, and if a job contains such tasks, it is vulnerable to computerization.

Outside such an occupation-level examination, it is exciting to drill down to specific jobs and consider how AI could change them. We have done this for the OINET Middle School

Teachers. The table lists certain of the teacher's jobs, as they are itemized in OINET, in their command of standing. The possible influence of AI on jobs is founded on the author's calculation and should be occupied as revealing. One elucidation might be that technology has currently progressed to a stage where also certain challenging human mental activities, such as executing tasks connected to education, managerial and communication tasks, can be done by computers. A more severe opinion might be that teachers are in the present educational systems loaded with somewhat motorized tasks. The list of high-importance jobs also reproduces profound opinions about the purposes of teaching and the social institutes around it. For instance, relative high-stakes analysis and valuation of accomplishment might be extremely vital if educational organizations are cast off for social selection. In educational systems that highlight growth and, for instance, social capabilities, the determinative valuation may be advanced in the list.

Artificial Intelligence capabilities and task substitution in the three-level model

If we make use of the three-level activity model, the econometric research of the future of jobs and demand for talent seems in an innovative light. As Von Neumann claimed around five decades ago, if we can precisely and unequivocally define a task, it is probable to plug-in a computer to execute the task.

Von Neumann was speaking regarding the competence of computers to pretend any system which can be replicated, though he also elucidated that we might require novel forms of judgment and new formalisms to carry this out. A humble deduction from this could be that there are no essential technical blockages that might create mechanization just a dream. Certainly, well-known writers like Bostrom and Kurzweil appear to accept such an opinion. In the background of the three-level model of human activity and cognition, the level of activity is not directly reachable for individual human reasoning. It offers an implicit traditional and social foundation that creates activities evocative. As Polanyi and Hayek, amongst others, have highlighted, ample of the knowledge that reinforces social action is contextual, dispersed, entrenched in social institutes and tools, and ratified in exercise. It appears, consequently, that this cultural and social coating can be merely partly enunciated and made clear.

If von Neumann was correct, and the whole thing that can be clearly labeled can be calculated, it appears that the level of acts and reasoning is the level where calculating could have it. This, certainly, is the level where majority logic- and knowledge-based Artificial Intelligence work has been done. In this opinion, the significant blockage is not practical; in its place, it is representative. Though we may transform some implicit knowledge to obvious knowledge, this needs a setting that unavoidably stays unstated.

An alternate method to resonate with the query of task replacement is, to begin with, the declaration by one of the prominent AI specialists, Andrew Ng. He sums up the competences of machine learning and neural AI in a compressed way:

"If a distinctive individual can do a cerebral activity in less than one second of mental reasoning, we can perhaps mechanize it by using AI either in the near future or now."

This highpoint the opinion that present neural AI and machine learning systems discourse the extreme stage of the three-level pyramid. Jobs that need pattern formation and reflex response are well matched for administered learning models. Nevertheless, there is a warning to Ng's description: What sums as a "typical" person? Many "less-than-one-second" human jobs need many months of learning.

Few of these, for instance, learning to walk, are somewhat behavioral, and could also be learned by AI-backed robots. Several of these jobs, conversely, also need long episodes of traditional and social space. It might, consequently, be probable, for instance, to use AI to pretend a performance pianist frolicking Bach's Goldberg variations and produce music that sounds alike. Expressive clarification of Goldberg variations, though, needs a wide knowledge about social history, the echo of the relation of Bach to other music makers, awareness about succeeding understandings, as well as the duration of training.

It might take a smaller amount than a second to play a tune, but it may well take several years to be capable of doing that. Though it is unblemished that a concert pianist might not be a "usual" person, several very typical ordinary jobs need parallel enculturation and wisdom. Certainly, a dominant assertion in Vygotsky's theory of cognitive development in the early 1930s was that those innovative intellectual abilities that separate humans from other creatures are precisely those abilities that cannot be defined as meek reflexes, but which need societal and social learning. This proposes that Ng is actually speaking about natural behavior in place of intellect. The major automation tailback, consequently, is not about technical ability. It is in the qualitative variance among pragmatic behavior and its connotation.

As soon as the gist of the action is static, we might be able to automate the behavior and acquire to do this by using a massive number of samples of such behavior. Several forms of human education and progressive forms of human reasoning, though, are founded on making sense where it was not afore. To discourse such zones of the human intellect, AI investigators will want models of understanding that far surpass those that are presently castoff in AI.

Trends and transitions

Econometric educations on the impact of computerization, automation, and Artificial Intelligence are therefore exciting and imperative; however, they do not estimate the future well. Overall terms, there is no clear motive why ancient tendencies would stay usable in socio-economic changes. Econometric models might be significant for accepting the current in light of the past; however, they can forecast the future only if no significant changes occur. This is only for these models that are data-based, and we don't have experimental data regarding the future. They are, though, significant for they propose that we can forecast the future in a fully precise way: If nothing significant changes, extensive use of currently prevailing AI technologies will suggest a future that will be dissimilar from what it had been.

This slightly inconsistent outcome displays that if, for nothing else, this is because paid labor used to be such a central factor in shaping the industrial age, its institutions, and our everyday life.

Neural AI as data-biased technological change

Fresh research by Quintini50 and Nedelkoska at the OECD delivers a decent appraisal of econometric research on the influence of computerization and spreads the Frey and Osborne research by using the output of the OECD Survey of Adult Skills (PIAAC). Nedelkoska and Quintini coordinated the mechanical blockages from Frey and Osborne to PIAAC variables on the labour market and job tasks, like rate of intricacy, problem-solving and counseling or educating others. The variables which were used by Nedelkoska and Quintini were very effective and purely contextual. For a sample of 32 countries, they established that the average job had 48 percent likelihood of getting computerized, with significant variations across countries.

Economists have employed skill-biased as well as task-biased models to investigate the influence of computerization, computers, and Artificial intelligence. Neural AI and ML, although, do not fit these models well. The serious blockage is not if a job is monotonous or non-monotonous, or if it needs compound problem solving; in its place, it is if the job could be learned by a machine.

This, in turn, relies on if there are statistics that could be used for learning. The influence of AI on jobs can, consequently, best be agreed in a "data-biased" model. If statistics are accessible and history recaps itself, present ML algorithms may at least in code feign the past. To the degree that learning, invention and knowledge formation is about uniting current pieces of knowledge, technologies may also be clever to do that. From a technical theme of view, such actions are decently syntactic. There are respectable reasons to anticipate that societal, economic, and intellectual process, as well as other systems that could be called living, cannot be counterfeited using such a method.

Education: a creator of capability platforms

As a result, AI might perhaps have its major influence when it is used to amplify human reasoning, and in assisting human knowledge and perception. This proposes a wide-ranging belief of keeping humans in the hoop when AI is used for scholastic purposes and in educational surroundings. Supposing that some jobs, maybe such as truck drivers, utility meter readers or data entry keyers, will turn out to be outdated in days to come, an imperative query for education policy is how folks in these jobs can transfer to fresh jobs. The Royal Bank of Canada (RBC) new research concentrated on this inquiry, finding six skill groups that could be used to cluster jobs in Canada.

Also, this research used OINET statistics but concentrated on skills in place of jobs as was thru in the Frey and Osborne research. The RBC research debated that as several jobs overlay in their skill requirements, it is comparatively stress-free to accompaniment skills inside these groups in techniques that allow people to transfer to fresh jobs when their old occupations grow automated. This method, thus, balances the opinion that there are main transversal talents and capabilities that are essential for the future.

Analogous questions might be requested for important capabilities as well-defined in the EU Key Competences for Lifelong Learning, and also for the European Framework for Digital Competence of Educators. We are going to talk about some example abilities which might have an influence on the main skill in languages. In general, research on future labor and skill demand propose that schooling cannot certainly an emphasis on precise work-related expertise in the future. In its place, education should generate capability stages that allow real life-long learning. Rather illogically, such an opinion on "platform education" proposes that we might be touching back again the medieval trivium54 and quadrivium55, along with their seven liberal arts. Business administrators have by now for a lot of years, reasoned that we want educational systems that show people grammar, rhetoric, logic, geometry, arithmetic. Though astronomy and music have not been tall on the list, maybe this is because they are now included in terms such as imagination and science.

Direct Artificial Intelligence impacts on advanced digital skills demand

The growth of advanced AI and ML models needs very tall points of capabilities in some areas. This is one of the motives why AI specialists are currently being salaried very high. The amount of neural AI specialists is maybe amplifying yearly, but the elementary understanding wanted for state-of-the-art exertion in this space needs cutting-edge levels of mathematical, scientific, and technical skills that are demanding to obtain. Expansion of advanced AI approaches needs a good understanding of linear algebra, statistics, differential equations, plus computer architectures as well as emergent chip technologies, and tools. The mandatory talent set is somewhat scarce, and fresh approximations put the number of folks with this set around tens of thousands. There are certain 5,000 individuals who have inscribed academic researches or offered at AI conferences in past years. It might be anticipated that the great discernibility of AI and the present demand will comparatively quickly direct aptitude to this area. As a sample, as its launch 2018, around 90000 scholars from above 80 countries have registered to the six-week Elements of AI – course organised as part of the AI Education programme by Finnish Center of AI.

This preliminary course has been widespread amongst legislators and in the public sector as well as private organisations who try to brand a sense of expansions in AI. High-level abilities in AI, though, cannot be learnt rapidly, and the shortage of AI-related talents might have grave unintended effects for instruction and learning. In 2017, AI connected commercial mergers and attainments were about 21.8 billion USD global, and start-ups deprived of revenue raised prices that sum to $5-10 million per AI professional. As highly-qualified specialists can now make very lucrative annual salaries, colleges will have excessive problems in finding capable teachers for this field. Certain applied application labor can be done by comparative trainees using openly accessible growth tools and learning resources, but the growth of mission-critical applications needs fairly innovative skills.

One somewhat instant outcome of this condition is that high-level AI aptitude and calculates competence will perhaps be delivered as a service. This might maybe mean that there is not going to be huge wants for high-level AI capabilities. Due to the elevated wage differences, many present scholars of statistics, mathematical physics, mathematics, computer as well as chip design, and maybe neurophysiology may, though, reassess their line of business paths and discover new identities as specialists in AI.

Furthermore, in the present relaxed learning setting, relaxed access to state-of-the-art technologies and exploration might also mean that high-level AI capabilities might arise from unpredicted places, for instance, through open hardware and open software groups.

Generally, AI can be used in three fundamentally dissimilar techniques that might have dissimilar effects for the growth of human reasoning abilities both in kids and grown-ups. First, AI can upkeep existing capabilities. When capabilities are agreed as blends of domain defined proficiency and behavioral ranges, Artificial Intelligence can decrease the necessity for human understanding, skill, and ability, and highlight the significance of behavioral ranges. As a consequence, humans do not essentially need to study domain explicit knowledge that previously was obligatory for experienced behavior. In specific, as domain-specific awareness turn out to be less imperative for ability, transversal and domain-independent universal abilities might turn out to be comparatively more vital.

CPSIA information can be obtained
at www.ICGtesting.com
Printed in the USA
BVHW091531250621
610374BV00004B/318